The Secret World of Oil

WITHDRAWN

Ken Silverstein

VERSO
London • New York

To Gabriel and Sophia, again.

The author would like to thank Open Society Foundations, where he was a fellow, for supporting the research that led to this book, and thanks also to Open Society's Justice Initiative. Thanks go as well to *Harper's*, *Foreign Policy*, *Slate*, the *New Republic*, and *Salon*, where parts of this book were previously published.

First published by Verso 2014
© Ken Silverstein 2014

1 3 5 7 9 10 8 6 4 2

Verso
UK: 6 Meard Street, London W1F 0EG
US: 20 Jay Street, Suite 1010, Brooklyn, NY 11201
www.versobooks.com

Verso is the imprint of New Left Books

ISBN-13: 978-1-78168-137-4 (HBK)
ISBN-13: 978-1-78168-783-3 (EXPORT)
eISBN: 978-1-78168-193-0 (US)
eISBN: 978-1-78168-645-4 (UK)

British Library Cataloguing in Publication Data
A catalogue record for this book is available from the British Library

Library of Congress Cataloging-in-Publication Data

Silverstein, Ken.
 The secret world of oil / Ken Silverstein.
  pages cm
  ISBN 978-1-78168-137-4 (hardback) — ISBN 978-
1-78168-193-0 (ebook) — ISBN 978-1-78168-645-4
(ebook)
 1. Petroleum industry and trade—Employees.
 2. Petroleum industry and trade—Corrupt practices. I.
Title.
 HD9560.5.S537 2014
 338.2'7282—dc23
                    2014000633

Typeset in Fournier by MJ & N Gavan, Truro, Cornwall
Printed in the US by Maple Press

Contents

Introduction
The Secret World of Oil

Most people think about oil as something pumped from the ground or used to make the gasoline that fills their fuel tanks. But between those two points, and beyond, a wide range of players takes a cut of the profits, from middlemen who broker deals between energy companies and government officials in countries sitting atop the world's energy reserves, to academics, lobbyists, and flacks whose incomes derive from their promotion of the fossil fuel economy.

This book will explore the secret world of oil and examine the little discussed but important role played by these various actors in the global fossil fuel economy. These fixers, traders, and lobbyists don't generally own nor operate oil refineries or wells; nevertheless, they smooth the workings of the energy business on the basis of discreet payments and backroom deals. They typically have excellent political contacts, which they can, when necessary, leverage into legal protection. Indeed, their success depends on their intimate connections to senior-level decision makers. "You have to deal with governments and ministers, and you have to service those people," one Swiss oilman told me. "You can call it corruption, but it's part of the system."

That's important to keep in mind, especially at a time when the global energy picture has been unusually bright. For much of 2013, for example, the US media was filled with upbeat news about America's energy situation. Thanks to new technology and higher prices, the energy industry was "extracting millions of barrels more a week, from the deepest waters of the Gulf of Mexico to the prairies of North Dakota," the *New York Times* said in a story early in the year. As a result the United States was moving closer to becoming independent from foreign energy sources of both oil and natural gas, "a milestone that could reconfigure American foreign policy, the economy and more."

Output was growing so quickly that the Energy Department reported that the US might overtake Saudi Arabia and become the world's largest producer by 2020, leading Congress to consider lifting a ban on exporting crude oil that was put in place after the Arab embargo of the 1970s. Meanwhile, Americans were driving less and buying more fuel-efficient cars, and hence using far less gasoline. "For decades, consumption rose, production fell and imports increased, and now every one of those trends is going the other way," Michael Levi, an energy and environmental senior fellow at the Council on Foreign Relations, told the *Times*.

This was deemed to be especially good news, because despite concerns about global warming, oil and other fossil fuels will remain the dominant source for the global economy for a very long time. Petroleum and natural gas will provide about half of America's total energy supply in 2030, according to the Energy Department, not significantly less than they do now. Furthermore, the US transportation network, and hence the broader economy, is overwhelmingly fueled by petroleum derivatives such as gasoline, diesel, and jet fuel.

And as a *Financial Times* article put it in September 2013, even as the US was "drowning" in oil, "the world has become, if anything, more dependent on a handful of Gulf producers to fill supply shortfalls"—oil production in Saudi Arabia, Kuwait, and the United Arab Emirates was at record levels. The article concluded:

> For all the talk about the shale boom, then, it is business as usual for the rest of the world in terms of supply. The concern remains, despite apparent nonchalance, that consuming nations like the US, China, and India will be stifled should production disruptions last.

In other words, oil and natural resource policy are as vital to global affairs as ever. Because of its financial weight and political significance, energy is the world's most important commodity and represents a $6 trillion annual market. Daniel Yergin estimates in his book *The Quest* that the value of the energy economy could increase by as much as 40 percent over the next twenty years, because of soaring demand, mostly from China, India, and other rising economic powers. And even with the surge in domestic production, the US (and its Western partners) will be importing oil and gas for decades to come, much of it coming from Third World countries with terrible records on human rights and corruption, among them Saudi Arabia, Nigeria, Iraq, Angola, Kuwait, Colombia, Azerbaijan, and Equatorial Guinea. As Dick Cheney once said, "The good Lord didn't see fit to put oil and gas only where there are democratic regimes friendly to the United States."

Whether the Unites States is exporting it or importing it, with oil some things never change. The political power of the energy industry, for example, remains as formidable as ever. Individuals and political action committees affiliated with oil and gas companies have collectively donated $238.7 million to candidates and the two parties (75 percent went to Republicans) over the past thirteen years, according to data from the Center for Responsive Politics. Between 2008 and 2012, they spent an average of about $150 million per year on Washington lobbying. Midway through the last year, oil and gas companies had spent more on lobbying than all but four other industries (the pharmaceutical sector was number one) and almost as much as Wall Street and defense combined.

The industry won huge favors during the administration of former oilmen George W. Bush and Dick Cheney but has fared quite well under Barack Obama as well. A piece that ran in 2013 on the *Forbes* magazine Web site, "Don't Worry Big Oil, President Obama Probably Doesn't Hate You As Much As You Think," noted that his administration had done much to help energy companies and had largely dismissed calls by environmentalists and others to regulate the industry.

Another constant in the energy business is corruption. Partly due to the political geography Cheney referred to, the energy industry violates the US Foreign Corrupt Practices Act more frequently than any other economic sector, even weapons makers. Two central figures in this secret world are fixers and traders. Fixers open doors for corporate clients and arrange introductions to the various potentates they know. They help companies navigate the local bureaucracy, or provide the lay of the land with political and economic intelligence, or point to important people or companies that should be courted or hired in order to curry favor. Fixers funnel money to dictators to obtain concessions for oil companies, set up shell firms and front companies to move money, and line up firms to explore for oil. In some cases, fixers feed money to those in power, in payoffs that often would be illegal under American and European antibribery laws.

Oil traders operate in a similarly murky world. They negotiate and purchase output from energy-producing nations, find buyers, and charter tankers to ship the oil. The original trader was Marc Rich, who during the 1970s and 1980s pioneered the practice of commodities swaps with outlaw regimes, frequently in war zones. In a profile, *Businessweek* reported:

> Rich is notorious for trading with Iran during the hostage crisis, South Africa during apartheid, and Cuba and Libya during US trade embargoes. In 1983 he fled to Switzerland after being indicted by the Justice Dept. for racketeering, trading with the enemy (Iran), dodging a $48 million corporate tax bill, and other violations that could have resulted in 300 years of jail time.

In 2001, Rich received a controversial pardon from President Bill Clinton on his last day in office.

The biggest oil trading firms are Swiss-based Glencore and Vitol. Given the enormous size of these companies—in 2011, Glencore was valued at $60 billion, higher than Boeing or Ford Motor Co.—and the global scope of their operations, remarkably little is known about them. In recent years, major oil-trading firms were discovered to have arranged secret deals with pariah states such as Sudan and were implicated in the United Nations oil-for-food scandal during Saddam Hussein's rule in Iraq. More recently, Amsterdam-based Trafigura, a trading firm that operates widely in West Africa, was found to have dumped four hundred tons of toxic waste in the Ivory Coast. The company paid a fine of nearly $200 million to settle charges stemming from the case, which resulted in ten deaths and tens of thousands of illnesses.

Third World countries have become more sophisticated and are better able to negotiate directly with oil companies, and the biggest multinationals are powerful enough that they sometimes operate without go-betweens. But fixers and traders continue to have utility. A worldwide scramble for oil is under way, with the United States and China being the two major competitors. There are fewer major fields and concessions available, and national oil companies control much of what's out there. That makes the stakes higher and the desperation to get in greater. Companies are always looking for an advantage, and often the right fixer or trader can be the means to gain it.

The lines of US anticorruption laws are drawn very strictly, but oil company executives are sent overseas to make deals, and they are measured by performance. Ed Chow, a longtime Chevron executive, told me, "You're supposed to be clean, but you're also supposed to create business. That leads to a tension, and a temptation to use middlemen. Let him do whatever he needs to do; I'm not part of it and don't want to know. In some ways, it's not that different from hiring lobbyists or giving campaign contributions. We just do it at home in a different way."

The process for awarding oil contracts and concessions in Third World countries is inherently politicized and centralized, because energy resources typically belong to the state and decision-making power is concentrated in the hands of a dictator or a small group, Chow explained. "In Texas, I can convince landowners to lease me their mineral rights. They get a royalty check every month and the companies leave a small footprint on their land. What's not to love? There is no equivalent in places like Nigeria or Angola or Kazakhstan. You get the land, but you don't provide a lot of jobs, you may be destroying the environment, and most of the profit goes to international capital. The companies don't have a strong case to sell to local communities, so they come to not only accept highly centralized government but to crave it. A strongman president can make all the necessary decisions. It's a lot easier to win support from the top than to build it from the bottom. As long as we want cheap gas, democracy can't exist."

The intimate ties between strongman presidents and multinational energy firms are another topic detailed in this book. Of particular note is General Teodoro Obiang Nguema Mbasogo, who has ruled the small West African nation of Equatorial Guinea since seizing power in a 1979 coup. The basis of the Obiang regime's wealth is oil, most of it pumped by American firms such as ExxonMobil and Hess Corporation. With an estimated output of about three hundred thousand barrels per day, Equatorial Guinea has emerged as the third-largest energy producer in sub-Saharan Africa.

For more than a decade, Obiang and his family members have spent enormous sums of money in the United States on real estate and extravagant purchases at stores such as Dolce & Gabbana and Louis Vuitton. In 2011, the American government finally acted to halt their collective shopping spree when it filed a civil asset forfeiture complaint seeking to take possession of tens of millions of dollars in assets owned by Obiang's son and heir apparent. The son, who is the country's minister of forestry, was alleged to have used money laundered through US banks to buy a $30 million estate in Malibu, a private plane, and assorted Michael Jackson memorabilia, including a "white crystal–covered 'Bad Tour' glove."

But Obiang and other oil-rich foreign leaders have few problems lining up support in Washington and typically have numerous lobbying and PR firms on retainer to peddle themselves to the American public and policy makers. Lobbying, though, is subject to disclosure laws, and hence in recent years foreign governments and interests seeking influence in Washington have increasingly turned to other means, which are largely unregulated and don't require public disclosure—which of course makes them all the more effective and useful.

These newer tactics include: making contributions to think tanks, universities, and nonprofit groups; setting up business associations that advocate for better political ties with the US but aren't legally defined as lobbying organizations; and offering huge consulting contracts and speaking fees to politically prominent Westerners—retired politicians (and their offspring), corporate titans, college professors, think-tank fellows, and countless former senior US officials, who use their experience and connections to promote the oil industry's interests in these countries and advocate for closer ties to the US.

For example, the departed Libyan leader Muammar Gaddafi recruited prominent academics and former officials through the Monitor Group of Cambridge, Massachusetts, which was charging his regime $250,000 per month to burnish its image. Among those the Monitor Group lined up—in exchange for big fees—were historian Francis Fukuyama, the Middle East scholar Bernard Lewis, neoconservative Richard Perle (who twice traveled to Libya for meetings with Gaddafi), and Professor Joseph Nye of Harvard, who also visited Libya and wrote a favorable story afterward for the *New Republic*. Nye also offered advice to Saif Gaddafi, the colonel's son, on the dissertation he wrote for the London School of Economics.

Gaddafi also counted on support from the Washington-based US-Libya Business Association, which was founded and funded by American oil companies. The group was headed by David Goldwyn, who worked at the Energy

Department under Clinton and who, after retiring from government to run a consulting firm that provided "political and business intelligence" to industry, returned to public service as the State Department's coordinator for international energy affairs during the Obama administration. A few others featured in this book include:

- Former British prime minister Tony Blair, who netted about $150,000 for a twenty-minute speech in Azerbaijan, in which he said that President Ilham Aliyev was a leader with a "very positive and exciting vision for the future of the country." A WikiLeaked cable offered a less flattering description of Aliyev, comparing him to Sonny Corleone, the fictional mobster from *The Godfather*.
- Neil Bush, the son of one American president and the brother of another, who one newspaper observed ran numerous business ventures that had "a history of crashing and burning in spectacular fashion." Nonetheless, Bush's family name has led various natural resource companies to hire him to broker deals in Asia and Africa.
- Bretton Sciaroni, a portly American and former ideologue of Ronald Reagan's White House who played a little-known but vital role in the Iran–Contra scandal but now resides in Phnom Penh, where he is an official adviser to Prime Minister Hun Sen, a one-time Khmer Rouge cadre, and opens doors for Western natural resource firms.

In large part because they inhabit the shadows of the energy world, the oil literature has largely consigned such middlemen and other characters to the margins of attention, or omitted them entirely. Yet it is precisely these sorts of friends that help the energy industry thrive and prosper, and this book for the first time puts them at center stage, where they belong.

1

The Fixers: Ely Calil

A lot of my business comes from someone who has a problem and who knows someone who knows me. Then the first someone gets directed to me and asks, "Can you fix it?"

—Ely Calil

On a cold, damp November night several years ago, a Mercedes sedan looped through the semicircular drive of the Saint James Paris, a century-old château-style hotel across the Seine from the Eiffel Tower. As the car rolled to a halt at the hotel's main entrance, a well-tailored, trim man named Ely Calil walked unhurriedly out the lobby door and down wide stone steps, talking into an earpiece that was connected, through a thin black wire, to a tiny cell phone tucked in the closed palm of one hand. The driver stepped from the car and opened the door for Calil, who interrupted his conversation to give the driver instructions. He spoke in a voice a little above a whisper, perhaps just a touch softer than his normal cool, flat tone. The driver returned to his seat and steered the car out through the granite-pillared entryway and onto Avenue Bugeaud.

That night Calil's destination was Spring, a popular restaurant in the ninth arrondissement that offers a set four-course menu to sixteen diners nightly. He was meeting Friedhelm Eronat, a close friend and sometime business partner who is equally reclusive and press-averse. Like Calil, he is one of the world's leading oil fixers, having grown rich brokering deals for Mobil (before it merged with Exxon) in Russia, Kazakhstan, and Nigeria. A confidential corporate due diligence report about Eronat that I obtained said that the precise nature of his relationship with Mobil was the "subject of much conjecture," but his contacts "went straight to the top." More recently he has done business in Argentina, Brazil, and China.

Calil had flown to Paris earlier that day from London, where he resides. Born in Nigeria in 1945 to a prominent family of Lebanese origin, Calil belongs to a small group of middlemen, a few dozen at most. They quietly arrange deals and financial transfers—not necessarily illegal—that are vital to the oil industry's operations. Calil has funneled money to African dictators to obtain concessions for oil companies, traded oil from Russia following the collapse of the Soviet Union, and advised presidents and exiled political leaders.

Along the way he has not only amassed an immense personal fortune but has established a web of political ties stretching from Africa to the Middle East and the United States. "He's built a very effective network of contacts and allegiances and loyalties through money and allowances," a former senior CIA official who has worked with Calil told me, not without admiration. "It's sort of like *The Godfather*. One day he'll come to ask for a favor, and you'll have to comply."

A former friend of Calil's, who broke with him over a business deal gone bad, spoke bitterly about him but conceded, "He's a lovable rogue and a very shrewd operator, there's no doubt about that."

A fixer's business demands discretion. "If you go and blab about your contacts, and talk about being a friend of the president, the next thing you know the president doesn't want to be your friend," one middleman told me. Calil, for his part, largely avoided publicity for most of his lengthy career. Although he is said to be one of the wealthiest men in Britain, and is a regular on the London club circuit, his name rarely surfaced in the press; for decades, the only photograph newspapers could find to accompany articles about him was a snapshot from his 1972 wedding to the American tobacco heiress Frances Condon, the first of his three wives. Little was known about the man himself, and the few news stories about him described him variously as "reclusive," "secretive to the point of obsession," and a businessman "whose privacy is guarded like a Mogul emperor."

However, in 2004 Calil became the subject of intense and unflattering press scrutiny. That year a group of about sixty South African and European mercenaries were arrested in Zimbabwe, where they were buying weapons. The men were said to be en route to Equatorial Guinea. It was a tale straight from *The Dogs of War*, and Obiang's regime and the alleged ringleader, Simon Mann, subsequently claimed that Calil had financed the coup plot in hopes of installing in power an exiled political leader named Severo Moto. The accusations have never been proven, and Calil vociferously denies he had any role in the affair. But the scandal that followed received worldwide publicity and embroiled well-known acquaintances of his, including Mark Thatcher, the son of former British prime minister Margaret Thatcher, and Lord Jeffrey Archer, whom scandal had twice forced to resign from parliament and who did prison time for perjury.

My acquaintance with Calil began two years before the alleged coup attempt, when I received a call from Victoria Butler, a Washington public-relations specialist who was then helping Moto meet with government officials and journalists. I'd written frequently about the Obiang regime, and so I went to see Moto at Butler's townhouse on Capitol Hill. He had already met with a number of Bush administration officials and members of Congress, and he expressed a naive optimism that the administration might eventually turn against Obiang because of his undeniably appalling human rights record.

As Moto and I chatted on a sofa, another man sat nearby in an armchair and scrolled through his e-mails on a BlackBerry. It was Calil, who told me that he and a number of other businessmen had sponsored Moto's trip and had retained Butler through a PR office. I had never heard of Calil, and when I returned home that day and used Google to try to find out more, I turned up little outside of a few small clips in European oil-industry publications. His name had briefly surfaced in a bribery scandal in France, where reports alleged that he funneled money to former Nigerian dictator Sani Abacha on behalf of Elf Aquitaine, a French oil company (which later was bought by a French competitor, Total).

Since that first meeting, Calil and I became unlikely friends. My family and I get together with him when he comes to Washington, and on a number of occasions I've visited him at his home in London. I've always liked Calil, and enjoyed his company, and appreciated the fact that he rarely tried to dress up his motives as altruistic, as oil company executives and industry players so often do. Oil had made Calil rich and that was why he was in the business.

By the time of his meeting in Paris with Eronat, the worst of the Equatorial Guinea–related publicity had blown over, and Calil had regained a measure of his preferred anonymity. I'd long wanted to profile him and having finally convinced him, was with him that night.

Eronat was awaiting us at a corner table when we arrived at the restaurant. Eronat used to live in a Victorian mansion down the road from Calil in London's Chelsea section but following an acrimonious separation and pending divorce, he was spending most of his time in Geneva and Paris, where he owns an apartment near the Saint James. He was waiting with his longtime partner, a tall, blond Russian attired in a dark dress and knee-length black boots, and her friend, Angelika, a Russian model who had dark hair and porcelain skin, and wore jeans, a white cotton shirt, and a dark vest. Whereas Eronat's partner was gregarious and chatty, Angelika, perhaps because of her halting English, sat quietly at the table and occupied much of her time checking text messages on her cell phone.

I had never met Eronat or seen his photograph, but based on his name I had envisioned a refined, stuffy Central European aristocrat. It turns out that he was born Romanian[1] but came with his mother to Louisiana when he was a young boy. Tall and hefty, he looked quite a bit younger than his fifty-five years, and was dressed casually, in light-brown corduroys and a tan pullover. Eronat studied petroleum engineering at Louisiana State University in the 1970s and got a job as an engineer after graduating, then went to work for an oil-trading firm before branching out on his own.

Eronat met Calil in the early 1980s, in Nigeria. "Ely was the man to see," Eronat recalled, after sampling a red wine and then ordering several bottles for the table. "Back then," he added, "it was a very small club, and we all knew one another. You did business by gentleman's agreement. When you called and said you had a cargo of crude, you confirmed the price and details over the phone. If your word wasn't honored, you were finished."

Eronat's own contacts in Nigeria were also strong. The due diligence report said his influence in the country was "based on his ability to sustain long-term relationships with key members of several Nigerian administrations," including military leaders and powerful civilians like Rilwanu Lukman, who in the 1980s was minister for petroleum and later was named secretary general of OPEC.

For years Calil and Eronat attended the twice-a-year meetings of OPEC oil ministers. "There were twenty regulars, if you want to be generous," Calil said. "You'd meet all the ministers and entertain them." Eronat pulled out his cell phone and showed me a picture from the 2008 meeting in Saudi Arabia of OPEC heads of state (which is one level up from the ministerial meetings). It was hard to make out much on the small cell phone screen, but I could just see a beaming Eronat, dressed in a Western business suit and surrounded by people in Middle Eastern garb.

The two men have partnered together numerous times, though "we never had anything in writing, Friedhelm and I, not once," Calil said of their dealings. One particularly profitable stretch involved exporting oil from Russia in the early post-Soviet days. Calil recounted that they had met many of the country's future oligarchs "when they were wearing funny suits and selling shoes and cigarette lighters."

The two men spoke of some old comrades who had fallen on hard times following the global market turmoil of the late 2000s. "They're all selling their yachts," Eronat said with a grim look. One mutual friend, an oligarch they called Sascha, "had $44 billion, and now he's down to a billion."

"It happens," Calil deadpanned.

The waiter brought a bouillabaisse, small plates of scallops in a truffle sauce, and veal loin with poached pear. Everyone agreed the food was delicious, but there were complaints about the "presentation." Calil and Eronat, serious gourmets, seemed particularly dismayed. The two men decided to head to the famous brasserie L'Ami Louis for a proper meal. (This would include more wine, a plate of potatoes baked with dollops of goose fat and topped with shaved garlic, foie gras, and toast and cornichons, scallops, and snails in butter and garlic.)

For years L'Ami Louis was a sort of headquarters for their mutual operations, and they reminisced about a dinner there in the mid-1990s when they hosted fourteen well-connected Russians. "It was just them and the two of us," Eronat recalled while we were still at Spring. "We ordered a bottle of wine, and then another and another"—he mimed guzzling directly from the bottle—"until the waiter just brought a case of wine and put it on the ground next to our table." It was an extraordinarily expensive meal, the two men recalled, but well worth it, in that it played an important role in advancing their Russia business.

Calil asked for the check before dessert was served and called L'Ami Louis from his cell phone. "You don't ask for a table, you just say you're coming," he said as he hung up.

The next morning, when I sat down for coffee with Calil and Eronat at the Saint James, Eronat was reading the *International Herald Tribune*. He folded the paper, pushed it my way, and pointed to a story: Spain's government was hesitating to allow the Russian company Lukoil to buy a controlling stake in Repsol YPF, Spain's largest oil firm. "Oil is not a commodity," Eronat said. "It's a political weapon."

"Absolutely," Calil said as picked up his espresso cup. "That's why the Americans made that stop in Iraq."

Eronat told me that there used to be "about forty people" who ran the oil-trading business. "The world got bigger, especially when the oil market boomed and the hedge funds came in, but it's still a pretty small group of people," he said.

Calil and Eronat spoke about a mutual friend of theirs named James Giffen, a New York business consultant who was charged by the US government with allegedly funneling more than $78 million to Nursultan Nazarbayev, the president of Kazakhstan. The money was said to come from fees paid to Giffen by American oil companies that subsequently won stakes in Kazakh oil fields. Giffen also gave Nazarbayev and his wife gifts, including his-and-hers snowmobiles and hundreds of thousands of dollars worth of jewelry. "Oil fields are a battleground," said Eronat. "If Jim had not been involved, other [non-American] firms would have gotten the contracts, and the loser would have been the US government."

The federal indictment of Giffen, who established close ties to governments in the former Soviet Union during the Cold War, alleged that Nazarbayev assigned him to negotiate deals with foreign oil companies seeking to invest in Kazakhstan after the country's independence in 1991. Giffen accompanied the Kazakh leader to Washington for meetings with American officials and in 1998 even assembled a team of political consultants to lobby the US government on Nazarbayev's behalf. "He was Washington's de facto ambassador to Kazakhstan," Robert Baer, a former CIA officer, told me.

Giffen never specifically denied funneling money to Nazarbayev but claimed his role and actions were fully known by the US government. A filing from his lawyers claimed that Giffen's acts might seem unusual, but that "imposing American domestic conceptions of honest services on all the world's governments" would "wreak havoc" on the workings of international law.

Calil, who had recently visited Giffen in New York, concurred. "Jim never worked for the CIA, but he continuously informed the CIA," he said, a line of argument that Giffen advanced in court. "He was never discouraged, and in fact was encouraged to have that relationship with Nazarbayev. You don't take him to court—you give him a medal."

The judge in the case, William Pauley, agreed. In late 2010, after the Justice Department dropped all bribery counts in exchange for a misdemeanor tax plea, Pauley imposed no jail time on Giffen, called him a Cold War "hero," and said the government should never even have brought the case. "He was one of the only Americans with sustained access to high levels of government in the region," Pauley said. "These relationships, built up over a lifetime, were lost the day of his arrest. This ordeal must end. How does Mr. Giffen reclaim his reputation? This court begins by acknowledging his service."

In 2002, Calil himself was arrested by French police and briefly jailed in connection with the payments of enormous commissions to Sani Abacha by a subsidiary of Elf Aquitaine. During a judicial investigation, Philippe Jaffré, a former Elf CEO, confirmed that the payments were made. "The Nigerian oil fields were extraordinarily profitable," he said. "There was no other way to reach a friendly agreement." Jaffré said, however, that Calil and two other

Lebanese intermediaries—Gilbert Chagoury and Samir Traboulsi—"apparently received more money than foreseen." By Jaffré's account, the three split $70 million among them for their role in moving the funds.

Despite a lengthy investigation, Calil was never formally charged in the affair (though a number of Elf executives were sent to jail for embezzling millions of dollars from the company). He acknowledged having received commissions from Elf in order to funnel payments to Abacha, saying, "From a strictly legal standpoint, there was nothing strictly illegal about it. It has become illegal now. The commissions I took from the French companies were sanctioned by the French Ministry of Finance. They had to declare the commissions on their taxes. If it's wrong, then arrest the minister of finance. Why are you arresting me? Was it legal? Yes. Was it moral? I don't know. But business isn't about not making money. I'm not a philosopher, but the law is there to be tested. If you're on the wrong side you should be sanctioned, and if you're not you should be left alone.

"Americans want their gasoline cheap," Calil added. "But it's not possible without cutting a few corners."

Among the thornier political issues surrounding oil is that most of it is extracted from undeveloped nations and shipped to rich ones, whose home companies pump it. Sometimes, a company will reach out to rulers of oil-rich states on its own, negotiating and striking deals with them through official emissaries. That's especially true of multinational giants such as ExxonMobil and Chevron, who have worked around the globe, in high-risk and low-risk countries, and can handle such matters on their own. "We were so damn big that we usually didn't need middleman," a former BP executive told me. "We worked directly with heads of states in the countries where we operated, and we could deliver [to those heads of state] geopolitical contacts back home that served their aspirations. When you're with BP, you can always arrange a meeting with the prime minister or tea with the Queen."

But often companies (including the giants) will instead work through men like Calil and Eronat: independent fixers, whose job it is to know the leaders and other government officials for whom oil serves as both piggy bank and political weapon. "Intermediaries can play a pivotal role in bridging the gaps of distance, time, custom and language between the corporate culture of the principal and the local business community," says a business guidebook prepared by TRACE International, which offers antibribery compliance advice for multinational companies.

> [But] the qualities that make an intermediary attractive to a company often are the same as those that make the relationship risky. Successful intermediaries are persuasive, well connected and tenacious. If the intermediary has no business advantages apart from personal connections, a more significant inquiry is warranted.

For international oil companies, working with fixers is only illegal if they are caught paying bribes or otherwise enriching foreign officials, but it requires careful due diligence. "Red flags go up any time you use a partner in an especially corrupt country, and especially if he is reputedly corrupt," says Homer Moyer, an attorney at the Washington firm of Miller & Chevalier and leading expert on the FCPA. "It's a little like unprotected sex. You're at the mercy of whom you get into bed with."

Fixers have always served an essential function in the oil business. The first to work on an international scale was Calouste Gulbenkian, a stateless Armenian Turk whose father was a banker and a major kerosene importer for the Ottoman empire. Known as "Five Percent" and the "Talleyrand of oil diplomacy," Calouste studied mining engineering at King's College in London, and upon graduation in 1887, was sent by his father to the Caspian port city of Baku to learn the oil trade. The young Gulbenkian wrote a series of scholarly articles that piqued the interest of the Ottoman Department of Mines. Officials there asked Gulbenkian to draw up a report on oil resources, and he pointed to several areas of great potential in the region. "Thus began Calouste Gulbenkian's lifelong devotion to Mesopotamian oil, to which he would apply himself with extraordinary dedication and tenacity over six decades," Daniel Yergin recounts in his definitive history of oil, *The Prize*.

Gulbenkian's fantastic success as an oil broker depended on his knowledge of the region and his cozy relationships— with Turkish officials, on the one hand, and with European and American oilmen on the other. In 1898, two years after he and his family fled the Armenian genocide, the Ottoman government appointed him financial adviser to its Paris and London embassies. In 1902, he obtained British citizenship, cementing his connection with the most powerful player in the partitioning of the Middle East. About a decade later, Gulbenkian helped broker a deal that led to the creation of the Turkish Petroleum Company, which was established to exploit Middle Eastern oil fields. The joint owners, which included Royal Dutch Shell, the National Bank of Turkey, and various German and British investors, granted him a 5 percent nonvoting share in the new company—hence Gulbenkian's nickname.

Sixteen years later Gulbenkian drew the map that defined a cooperative agreement among the French, Dutch, British, and Americans—their governments and companies—to extract oil from the former Ottoman territories. This Red Line Agreement earned him the bulk of his fortune, and his success established the model of the independent, cash-dispensing oil fixer.

The modus operandi was simple and straightforward: The fixer took money from a company seeking an energy concession, kept one part for himself, and funneled the rest into a Swiss bank account belonging to foreign officials, who awarded the concession. When the officials got their money, the fixer's sponsor got its contract. "For years you could not operate in many oil-producing countries without an agent, especially in the Middle East," Willy Olsen, a former senior executive at Norway's Statoil, told me. "If you had the wrong agent, one without the right connections, you were not relevant at all."[2]

Today fixers still play a vital role for oil companies in their dealings with heads of state and other government officials who, in the delicate phrasing of Laurent Ruseckas, an international energy analyst in London, "don't know how to commercialize their power." But although straight-forward cash bribes are still employed, the means of the payoff have become more complex. Partly this is for legal reasons. The United States outlawed bribery abroad in 1977, when the FCPA was passed. The Organization for Economic Cooperation and Development passed similar rules in 1997; until then, many European countries allowed their firms to deduct bribes on corporate income-tax state-ments. With the heightened legal risk, the greater public scrutiny of international business, and the more sophisti-cated government methods of monitoring bank transfers, payoffs now take a multitude of forms. Indeed, while as opaque as before and serving the same purpose, modern-day payoffs are not always illegal. "I spent 99 percent of my time trying to figure out ways to not technically violate the FCPA," a former Mobil executive in Angola once told me.

"Corruption isn't endemic in the energy business because people in the industry are more corrupt or have lower morals but because you're dealing with huge sums of capital," Keith Myers, a London-based consultant and former BP executive, told me. "A million dollars here or there doesn't make any difference to the overall econom-ics of a project, but it can make a huge difference to the economics of a few individuals who can delay or stop or approve the project."

Given the profits involved in the energy business, some-times even a few hundred million dollars doesn't make much of a difference. In February 2012, Jack Stanley, a former senior executive at Halliburton, was sentenced to two and a half years in prison after pleading guilty to charges involving bribes paid to Nigerian officials to win a mammoth energy project in that country. The story dates to 1995, when a four-member international consortium that included Houston-based M. W. Kellogg, a firm that Halliburton later bought, was awarded the first of three contracts to build a natural gas plant in Nigeria. That same year the consortium hired a British lawyer named Jeffrey Tesler, who had ties to senior Nigerian officials, to handle the natural gas plant business.

Over the next five years the consortium paid $176 million to Tri-Star Investments, a Gibraltar-based firm established by Tesler. That money was routed to Tri-Star through a company set up by the consortium on the Portuguese island of Madeira. It's not clear where all of that money went, but Tesler is believed to have kept a relatively small part of it and used the rest to pay kickbacks to Nigerian officials. It was a lot of bribe money but still very little compared to the nearly $6 billion in contracts that the consortium received as part of the natural gas project.

Tesler was extradited to the US and also sentenced to prison time for two counts of breaking foreign bribery law. "I allowed myself to accept standards of behavior in a business culture which can never be justified," he told the court in Houston at that time. "I accepted the system of corruption that existed in Nigeria. There is no day when I do not regret my weakness of character and being caught up in a violent military culture with customs that are harmful to the social fabric and breach of laws."

Edward Chow, a former Chevron executive who spent more than three decades in the oil business, described to me the logic by which intermediaries thrive. The process for awarding oil contracts and concessions in Third World countries is inherently politicized and centralized, he explained, because mineral resources typically belong to the state and decision-making power is concentrated in the hands of a dictator or a small group: "In Texas, I can convince landowners to lease me their mineral rights. They get a royalty check every month, and the companies leave a small footprint on their land. What's not to love? There is no equivalent in places like Nigeria or Angola or Kazakhstan. You get the land, but you don't provide a lot of jobs, you may be destroying the environment, and most of the profit goes to international capital. The companies don't have a strong case to sell to local communities, so they come to not only accept highly centralized government, but to crave it. A strongman president can make all the necessary decisions. It's a lot easier to win support from the top than to build it from the bottom.

"The question becomes how you reach the key decision makers—and that's where middlemen come in. You're looking to increase your access vis-à-vis the competition, and retaining the right fixer may be the best vehicle. You think, If this guy can get us the appointment and get to the decision makers—and usually they are just a handful at most—then it's worth spending the money, no matter what you have to pay. In some ways it's not that different from hiring lobbyists or giving campaign contributions. We just do it in a different way."

Although bribery and other payoffs have undeniably been part of the fixers' trade, the best are far more than bagmen to dictators. "There's a real art to acting as an agent, and the role differs from country to country," Robin Bhatty, an energy industry analyst, told me. "In most of the world, business is done on a personal basis. The best way of getting something done is finding someone who knows someone who you want to know, and you use them to make introductions." ("Just the same way you're calling me now," he added, after I asked him to put me in touch with some energy industry officials I was hoping to interview.)

Because oil fixers play such an important and sensitive role, they can accumulate extraordinary power with heads of state, who often bestow on them the title of presidential adviser and grant them use of a diplomatic passport. "Trading in weapons is trading in sovereignty," says Philippe Vasset, editor of the Paris-based newsletter *Africa Energy Intelligence*. "If you don't have them, you can't defend your borders. It's the same with oil, which gives you the liberty to run your ships and planes and tanks, and your economy. If you don't have it, you can't run your country."

Key brokers who emerged in the post-1973 OPEC world included: Marc Rich, who founded the giant commodities firm Glencore (see Chapter 3); Hany Salaam, a Lebanese middleman who made numerous deals for Occidental Petroleum Corporation during the days of Armand Hammer, its former chairman; and Oscar Wyatt, a Houston oilman and corporate raider who was sentenced to a year in prison in 2007 in connection with the UN oil-for-food scandal.

One of the more colorful of that era's fixers was John Deuss, who once owned his own tanker fleet, and who during the 1980s smuggled vast quantities of oil to South Africa's apartheid regime, then under an international trade embargo imposed by the United Nations. In 1979, after the overthrow of the shah, Iran stopped exporting oil to South Africa's apartheid regime, due to the embargo. Using fake documents and transferring oil from one tanker to another on the high seas, Deuss smuggled more than one hundred million barrels of crude to South Africa over the next four years.

"Guests invited to one or another of his residences found John Deuss to be a supremely hospitable host," writes Steve LeVine, author of *The Oil and the Glory: The Pursuit of Empire and Fortune on the Caspian Sea.*

> He often flew them in, aboard a pair of luxury Gulfstream jets, or ferried them around the Caribbean ... on Fluertje, a 150-foot yacht large enough for formal dinners on deck.

One oil industry veteran told me of Deuss: "You'd go to him and say, 'I need to see three people for a deal I'm working on.' He'd charge enormous fees, but he'd bring those three people to his home in Los Angeles and you'd meet them."

Homegrown fixers have emerged in Third World countries in recent years and become giants of the business. A major player in African energy markets is Samuel Dossou-Aworet, who was the longtime oil and financial adviser to Gabonese president Omar Bongo, who took power in 1967. Swiss and American investigators found that Dossou had opened accounts for Bongo at Citibank's private banking department in Paris and the Canadian Imperial Bank of Commerce in Geneva. A 1999 Senate report on money laundering indicated that in total Bongo had $130 million deposited with Citibank's private banking department.

Citibank officials set up accounts for Bongo in the name of Tendin Investments. In a November 6, 1998, e-mail, one bank executive warned of dire consequences of closing the Bongo accounts, even if they held corrupt proceeds.

> Whatever internal considerations we satisfy, the marketing fallout is likely to be serious. Sam [Dossou] gets his marching orders from Tendin. Tendin has been vitally instrumental in our franchise's success over the years … Sam helped the Branch considerably over the last two years to obtain a more reasonable and rightful share of public sector deposits, with Tendin's blessing.[3]

Dossou now runs a Monaco-based firm called Petrolin that reportedly markets the Gabonese government's share of oil exports. According to his bio on the Petrolin Web site, Dossou has "provided strategic input in the development of prominent oil companies and government entities" in more than a dozen countries, from Egypt to South Africa. "Dossou is trusted because he's got twenty years of unbridled reliability," says a First World oil consultant who has worked with him. "He's good to his word, even if it costs him, and in Africa that's worth a lot."

Before the fall of Muammar Gaddafi, London-based Mohammed Ajami, brother of the prominent Lebanese writer Fouad Ajami, helped companies looking for business in Libya. His utility to oil companies was based on his close relationship with the country's intelligence chief, Musa Kusa.

Another key Gaddafi-era fixer was Jack Richards, an American based in London who operated through a British Virgin Islands–registered firm, and who developed a close friendship with Libya's ruling family. The *Guardian* newspaper uncovered a 2005 memo written by one of Richards's oil industry clients, Petro-Canada (now Suncor Energy), which said that he had been based in Tripoli in the 1960s when he was working for the American communications company RCA and gave English lessons to a number of young army officers, including, as luck would have it, one named Muammar Gaddafi. The memo said:

> After the 1 September 1969 coup [which brought Gaddafi to power], Richards suddenly discovered that his students now occupied many of the most prominent positions in the country. It is alleged that he was [later] responsible for obtaining prime exploration blocks for one of the foreign oil companies now in Libya.

The *Guardian* story, which was published in 2011, said that Richards had taken Saif Gaddafi shooting on Princess Anne's estate and that his daughter had helped research Saif's PhD thesis at the London School of Economics. "I may have given advice to some people at one time but … I think I hadn't travelled to Libya for some years even,"

Richards told the *Guardian*. As for Saif, he said, "The more I see of him the more disappointed I am in him and what he's doing in that country."

I was able to see some of a fixer's work firsthand when Calil brought me along to a meeting with a New York hedge fund whose offices overlooked Park Avenue just south of Grand Central Station. Calil and a few of his associates gathered around a conference table with the fund's two bosses, whose names I agreed to withhold. One was American, neatly groomed and dressed, with the personality of an accountant; the other was Austrian, and he did most of the talking. The Austrian wore blue jeans and a white dress shirt with a few buttons undone, and his hair was wild, like Einstein's. Eccentric, arrogant, and utterly obnoxious—all traits that no doubt served him well in directing the hedge fund—he was flying off to St. Tropez the next day for a dental appointment.

The Austrian began the meeting by telling Calil and his associates a little bit about the fund. He explained how (no doubt for tax purposes) the firm's myriad assets were "ring fenced" in Panama, Luxembourg, and the British Virgin Islands, with separate contracts to operate each property. Its holdings included a boot factory in China and 150,000 hectares of Brazilian rain forest, he said, though when I asked him where the property in Brazil was, he had no idea. The fund also had bought two defunct oil refineries, and these acquisitions were to be the subject of the day's meeting. Because the refineries were quite old and could process only very dirty crude, few countries would allow them to operate today. When the fund took over the refineries it believed it had buyers who would reassemble them elsewhere, but the deals fell through. Now both of the refineries were crated up, and in one case the hedge fund had a contract requiring that the refinery be removed in a matter of months.

The fund had hundreds of millions of dollars tied up in these two refineries, so they were calling on Ely Calil for his expertise in unloading them. It was just the sort of challenge, and potentially huge payoff, that Calil relished. "I like to take on deals with 15 or 20 percent chance of success," he had explained to me a few days earlier. "If the odds are 1 percent, it's not worth my while, and if they're 50 percent, it's not that interesting, because there are two thousand people who can do it, so why would they pay me $15 million to do it?"

As he and the Austrian discussed the problem, a curious negotiation began to take place. The latter took great pains to stress how trifling this matter was to him; if Calil could help, then great, his tone implied, but otherwise he had many ways to resolve the situation. Calil clearly saw through this pose but did his admirable best to remain polite.

"Perhaps it's just my fatalism," he began, "but it's not going to be easy to sell the refineries." He pointed out that few countries today could possibly accept refineries so noxious. Angola had potential, he said, but the country was so corrupt, and its bureaucracy so complicated, that a deal would be hard to strike. Nigeria was, in theory, another option, but again the politics were complex. "You'd need to find a state governor to support the project, and it's possible that that could be arranged, but you also already have all the turmoil in the Delta region," which added, he said, an additional political complication.

The Austrian insisted that he already had a number of possibilities in play, and that he even had a "process" whereby he was evaluating those possibilities. He mentioned Pakistan in particular: "We have government support in Pakistan. They can change the government three times, I don't care. For me this new guy is better than the last one." But he acknowledged that a refinery there would be in constant danger of having its profits seized by the unstable government. "You have 170,000 starving people, and you don't want them all running to Islamabad," he said. "If you have an economic crisis and food prices are climbing, the government might step in and say to the owner, 'You can only take a 2 percent profit.' Maybe even for a few years you'd have to take no profit as a 'contribution' to the country."

"Through your process and my fatalism," Calil replied, "we've reached the same conclusion." Of course the hedge fund didn't really have an easy option in Pakistan, or anywhere else, and so it needed his help—for which he could command a steep price. Calil laid out a rough plan for how he might place at least one of the refineries. He had identified a potential spot in Lebanon, in the port city of Tripoli. An old refinery there had been shut down about thirty years ago; it was fed from a pipeline that originated in Kirkuk and ran through Syria. Now that the Iraqi government wanted to ship oil from Kirkuk again, Calil went on, Lebanon might be persuaded to site a refinery in the same spot. Of course, the hedge fund would need political support, but

fortunately, Calil said, he knew the Lebanese energy minister, and also had political contacts in Syria and Iraq. The
fund would also need petroleum engineers to work at the
Tripoli site, but Calil had just such a team at the ready, a
group of twenty-three Bosnian Muslims with whom he'd
worked before on a project in China. As mosque-going
Muslims, he pointed out, they were less likely to be shot
at or kidnapped in Tripoli. It was agreed that within the
month, Calil would take a delegation from the fund to
Lebanon for meetings with the relevant players.

Later that day, after we left the meeting, Calil talked a
little more about this deal, and how he happened to be so
well situated to help the hedge fund out of its dilemma.
"A friend of mine became energy minister in Lebanon—a
good friend," he recalled. "I said to him, 'Congratulations.
What sort of energy opportunities are there in Lebanon?'
We were just chatting. He mentioned that they hoped to
get the Iraqi oil pipeline reopened, that that would solve
a lot of economic problems. Just knowing that they are
looking at that refinery: that knowledge is wealth in itself.
You have that knowledge in your head. You also know that
Syria imports so much, and Lebanon imports so much,
and that the Syrians are talking to the Iraqis about opening
the pipeline. All that knowledge provides a theoretical
solution."

He added: "You also need connections to deliver the
solution—to influence the president, the prime minister,
the relevant ministers. That is about relationships. If you
don't know the person directly, you know his cousin or
someone close to his cousin."

In this case, I asked him, how big a problem would it be to get the political support?

"As big as I want it to be," he replied.

Calil said that approaching the Syrian government in the right fashion was essential: "If [the Austrian] goes in and says, I've come to increase the GDP of Lebanon by 5 percent, they'll say, 'Oh great, tell me more,' and make sure it never happens. I obviously start off by saying I'm doing something that's good for Syria. The key is distribution. You go to the important players and tell them this project will refine 150,000 barrels, and they know that part of that will go to their family or clan. Some of these refined products are in high demand, so being the distributor can make you good money. Forget about the profit from the refinery, this is just from the by-products."

Until 2006, Calil resided at Sloane House, a Chelsea estate he owned.[4] Perched behind gates of white stone, the estate was staffed to the hilt with servants and tastefully stocked with antique furniture, leather-bound books, and numerous busts of Napoleon, Calil's hero. One Sunday afternoon I sat with him in his study and listened to him take phone calls, his patter seamlessly switching from Arabic to French to English and back again. There was a Libyan official who told Calil that Muammar Gaddafi wanted to host a future World Cup soccer tournament in Tripoli and was hoping to establish his bona fides in the meantime by sponsoring a minitournament. Could Calil help arrange for the Senegalese national team to take part? A call to an official in Senegal followed, as did a conversation with a well-connected friend in Lebanon about a brewing political crisis there. Several visitors dropped by, including a pencil-thin, dour man from Glencore who grew more dour still when I was introduced as a journalist.

Calil was born in the Nigerian town of Kano, where his Lebanese parents settled in the 1920s. George Calil had prospered in Africa through a small business empire that was based on the cultivation of peanuts (for consumption and groundnut oil) but also included aluminum and small manufacturing. At an early age, Ely was sent to Lebanon and was privately educated there and in Europe. After his father died of stomach cancer in 1966, Ely—who has five sisters and a younger brother—was chosen to return to Nigeria and restructure the family business. He established close connections with government officials, becoming especially friendly with the transportation minister. At the time Nigeria was looking for a firm to help its hajj pilgrims get to Mecca; during one meeting the minister asked Calil if he knew anyone at Lebanon's Middle East Airlines. He said: "The joke of it was that my brother-in-law's sister was going out with a guy who was high up in the MEA hierarchy. She later married him. So I went to Beirut and met his boss, who was very interested. 'Do you really know the minister?' he wanted to know. He made a huge proposal, and at the end Middle East Airlines got a lot of business and Nigeria was able to transport out its hajj pilgrims in style. We had been making a few hundred thousand dollars here and there, but on this deal alone I made a few million dollars. I thought: 'Screw crushing peanuts to make oil.' This was as easy as putting two people together who needed each other."

Later, his friend became the minister of telecommunications, and he asked Calil to recruit companies to invest in Nigeria. "I learned a lot from him; he was very clever," Calil said. He recounted how he once had the minister at his home in Nigeria, along with an English businessman who was seeking a contract to lay telephone cables. By way of denigrating his chief competitor, a Japanese firm, the Englishman talked about having been tortured during World War II at a Japanese POW camp.

"As he was talking, the minister started taking off his tie, and then his jacket, and then his shirt—and there were whip marks on his back, scars. 'You know who gave these to me?' he asked. 'Two British police who arrested me when we were fighting for our independence. And you know what? I don't bear a grudge. I'll do business with the British as long as you give me the right price. So don't give me your political propaganda, just give me a good contract.'"

After the first OPEC oil shock, in 1973, Calil became seriously involved in the petroleum business, first trading oil and then obtaining concessions and reselling them. Within five years, oil had become the largest sector of his business. Calil's influence and wealth soared after the Nigerian general Ibrahim Babangida assumed power in a 1985 coup. When I asked Calil about his relationship with Babangida, who is still a power broker in Nigeria, he acknowledged that they were close friends. "I took his kids on holidays and to stay with me in London," he said. "He saw me as a sound independent adviser, not a sycophant. He asked me to handle a lot of back-channel communications, and he sent me out as an adviser to other African governments."

But Babangida was forced out in the face of popular protests in 1993 and ceded power to a civilian government.
Three months later, after Sani Abacha took power; his
regime earned worldwide condemnation by hanging an
activist named Ken Saro-Wiwa and eight other democracy
campaigners. Base Petroleum, a firm of Calil's that owned
several oil concessions in Nigeria, paid Washington lobbyist Robert Cabelly nearly four hundred thousand dollars
between mid-1996 and early 1997 to lobby the Clinton
administration on Abacha's behalf.

Gilbert Chagoury, a key fixer who is also of Lebanese
descent, worked in tandem with Calil in Nigeria. He was
especially close to Abacha and received oil concessions and
large-scale government construction contracts during his
rule. Cabelly, Calil, and Chagoury met with a number of
senior Clinton administration officials, including Susan
Rice, who then served on Clinton's National Security
Council and later as Barack Obama's UN ambassador and
national security adviser. During the lobbying campaign,
Chagoury contributed $460,000 to a Miami-based voter
registration group that was tied to the Democratic National
Committee. In December 1996, he and Calil attended a
White House holiday dinner with President Clinton for
top Democratic National Committee donors. "We were
getting traction, and we said we could bring him [Abacha]
around," Calil recalled. "But in the end he went off the rails,
and we had to walk away. It didn't matter what you did or
how much you paid, you couldn't gloss over the reality."

Abacha, who funneled several billion dollars into Swiss
accounts during his years in power, died in 1998 (reportedly

in the company of two prostitutes). Several years later a newly elected Nigerian government identified Chagoury as a key financial intermediary for Abacha. According to a *Wall Street Journal* account, Chagoury cut a deal in which he returned as much as $300 million to the Nigerian government in exchange for a written agreement that he would not be prosecuted. He still could have faced prosecution in several European countries, but that threat was preempted when the island state of St. Lucia named him as its ambassador to UNESCO, which gave Chagoury diplomatic immunity. Chagoury later made a comeback in Nigeria, and by the mid-2000s was again receiving major construction projects. Ironically, his chief backer was identified in news accounts as Ahmed Tinubu, a former governor who had made his name in politics as an anti-Abacha activist. His financial arrangements with Chagoury were not disclosed, but a local magazine reported that Tinubu had recently flown to Paris on Chagoury's private plane.

Chagoury has a mansion in the Los Angeles area and also had plenty of powerful friends in the United States. He's one of the biggest donors (between $1 million and $5 million) to the Clintons' foundation and appears to be a close friend of Bill's. Chagoury helped arrange a $100,000 speaking engagement for Bill Clinton, and in 2006 attended his sixtieth birthday party and, the following year, his aide Douglas Band's wedding in France.

Following the election in 1999 of Olusegun Obasanjo, who had been jailed for speaking out against the human rights abuses and corruption of the Abacha regime, Calil's influence in Nigeria waned. (Although when in power,

Obasanjo headed a government that proved pervasively corrupt itself.) But by then his scope of operations had expanded enormously. He became a confidant to Denis Sassou Nguesso, who had taken power in a 1997 civil war in the nearby Republic of the Congo. "Calil became the country's main oil adviser," said Philippe Vasset, of *Africa Energy Intelligence*. "All the traders courted him in order to get contracts."

Calil served as a personal adviser to Senegalese president Abdoulaye Wade, who won office in 2000.[5] Calil had befriended Wade when the latter was living in exile in Paris. He provided Wade with an apartment, introduced him to French government officials, and generally promoted him in political and media circles. Wade's base of operations while in exile was at the Paris offices of Saga Petroleum, a small Norwegian firm run by a friend of Calil's.

Calil also became the chief oil adviser to Idriss Deby, a warlord who had seized power in 1990 (and still holds it) in Chad. He was tasked with recruiting oil companies to develop projects in that country, and he himself, in conjunction with Eronat, landed a huge exploration concession there roughly the size of Texas. In 2003, the two men sold a major stake in the concession to China in a deal sealed, according to a report in the *London Evening Standard*, at a celebratory banquet thrown at Eronat's estate in Chelsea.

"You'd have an African head of state who would want advice—they all wanted oil to happen in their country," Calil explained to me of his work on the continent. "Of course you offered the advice pro bono, but you used that to build your network. Now it's considered a sin to do that.

They'd say, 'Look at this piece of land and see if it's worth anything.' And you'd go to Exxon and get them interested, and you'd sell them a part, and you'd keep the juiciest part of the concession for yourself. Everyone was happy. The president was happy because Exxon was now exploring for oil, Exxon was happy, and you had the heart of the concession. If you hadn't been there as the catalyst, the thing wouldn't have happened. You might call it abusing my role. I call it creating entrepreneurial wealth, and I created a lot of wealth."

When I asked him about his sensitive role as adviser to various African presidents, Calil downplayed the significance: "In Africa, to say 'thank you' they give you a diplomatic passport, because you backed their campaign or out of friendship. And then they'll introduce you in semi-official circles as their adviser. If I took you to some of these banana republics, on the third visit you'd be appointed as the media adviser. I've held the title of adviser, and the diplomatic passport, and I've given advice, but I've never had a desk at the presidential palace."

Africa has always been the main focus of Calil's operations, but he's done business around the globe. In addition to operations in Russia and the Middle East, he owned a Houston-based firm called Nautilus, which obtained oil and gas concessions in South America and Central Asia. He sold Nautilus to Ocean Energy, which subsequently was bought by Devon Energy, now the largest US-based independent oil and gas producer. Calil also won a gas concession in Brazil, which he later sold to Enron. Calil told me: "When buying and selling oil concessions, you're dependent on your skills and knowledge, but you're also very much dependent on the goodwill of the local government, from presidents to ministers. You end up building a political network to a) build up the business and b) protect it."

Calil's social and political networks are astonishing in scope. When I traveled to Sudan on a reporting trip, Calil supplied me with a cell phone number for one of the country's most senior intelligence officials. In Lebanon, I dined with Calil at the mountainside estate of Nayla Moawad, a government minister and powerful Christian politician.[6] He is a close friend of Mohammed Al-Saleh, the brother-in-law of King Abdullah II of Jordan, and of a number of Eastern European oligarchs, including the Russian Oleg Deripaska and Alexander Mashkevitch of Kazakhstan, both of whom appear on *Forbes* magazine's list of the world's billionaires. "He has the ability to get things done, just about anywhere," said a former CIA official of his post-agency business dealings with Calil. "We once needed an answer to a question in Syria, which is a very tough place to work. One of his associates talked his way into the deputy foreign minister's office and got us the information we were looking for."

Another former CIA officer now in business has also turned to Calil for help from time to time: "I've not found the country yet in the Middle East or Africa where we needed help where Ely couldn't reach out to someone of consequence, from sub-Saharan Africa to North Africa to the Gulf to the Levant. Before he does business in the country, he makes sure that he's got a network in place to safeguard his operations. He knows how to cultivate people with business, financial, political, and intelligence horsepower."

In the United States, Calil has relationships with both major political parties and contacts at the State Department and the CIA. "The minute you get anywhere in the oil business, the US system becomes interested," Calil told me. "The embassy invites you over, and the attaché wants to know what you're doing, and it builds from there. People tell you that you should meet someone, whether to impress you or please you or use you, and then it becomes a chain. There's nothing sensitive about knowing people; it's a talent, at the end of the day."

In Britain, Calil is a friend and longtime business adviser to Lord Archer, the writer and former deputy chairman of the Conservative Party. He is also close to Baron Peter Mandelson, a key figure in the British Labour Party and currently secretary of state for business, enterprise, and regulatory reform. Calil's closest social companions in London include the Syrian-born billionaire Wafic Said, who made his fortune through construction deals in Saudi Arabia and once helped broker a mammoth sale of British warplanes to Riyadh.[7]

Robin Birley, another close friend, runs an empire of London's most exclusive private clubs that was founded by his father, the best known of which is Annabel's. I visited Birley at his apartment on Brampton Square on a cold, cloudy afternoon. He was dressed in a dark sweater and slacks and smoking a cigar on a balcony when I arrived, and after buzzing me into the building, led me to a sitting room on the second floor. Glowing logs were piled high in a fireplace, and two whippets were comfortably situated, one on a sofa, where Birley took a seat, and the other on an armchair. "I hate the man but I love the piece," Birley said when he saw me admiring a large bust of Lenin on a table next to the fireplace.

Birley's face was disfigured when as a child he was mauled by a tiger at the private zoo of a family friend; his right eye remains slitted. He met Calil in the 1970s, when the latter was "a core member of the Birley clubs." In 1986, Birley's brother Rupert disappeared and apparently drowned while swimming near his home off the coast of Togo; his body was never found. Calil, who was a close friend of Rupert's, helped organize a search and provided a plane for the effort.

Birley is an ardent conservative: When Chile's former dictator, Augusto Pinochet, came to England in 1998 in order to avoid extradition to Spain to face charges for human rights violations, Birley helped coordinate a PR campaign on his behalf and financed his stay at the Wentworth Estate outside of London. But despite knowing Calil for three decades, he said they'd never discussed politics. "I assume he's conservative, but I don't really know," he said as he petted the whippet. "There are certain friends you can talk about anything with. With Ely there's an upper floor you can't get to. He's quite secretive and self-contained. I've never seen an outburst."

As to business, Birley described Calil as "ambitious and restless" and always in search of a big project. "It's not so much the money; he wants to build something on an imperial scale," Birley said. "He's not just an average businessman who buys and sells. He's more a Roman than a Carthaginian in that sense. He's a seriously clever man."

Calil was amused when I later told him what Birley had said about his "imperial" thinking. "Beyond a certain point," he said with a broad grin, "where you are able to eat and drink and buy a car or two, there has to be something more interesting that motivates you, whether it's the challenge itself or the end goal."

Calil has acknowledged being a friend and financial supporter of Severo Moto, the exiled political leader he is accused of seeking to put in power via the attempted 2004 coup in Equatorial Guinea. In return, Calil and others who allegedly backed the overthrow would have been given preferential rights to Equatorial Gunea's oil reserves by Moto's government.

The plot unraveled when a plane carrying over sixty mercenaries were arrested in Zimbabwe and charged with attempting to buy weapons for the alleged coup. (The mercenaries initially claimed they were buying the weapons for a mining project in the Democratic Republic of Congo.) A number of the men were extradited to Equatorial Guinea, including Simon Mann, who was also a former British army officer. They were taken to the notorious Black Beach prison, where they were beaten and tortured. Mann, the alleged coup leader, confessed to involvement in the plot and was sentenced to thirty-four years in jail.

In 2009, President Obiang pardoned Mann on "humanitarian grounds." Obiang is not known for his humanitarian impulses, and there was some suspicion that Mann cut a deal to get released. He was soon back in England singing the praises of dictator Obiang and charging that Calil had been a mastermind of the failed plot.

Calil had once unsuccessfully sought to do business in Equatorial Guinea, but nothing came of his overtures. Whatever happened, he and Obiang became bitter enemies in the aftermath.

He says he met Moto a few years prior to the coup, at a dinner party at a friend's home in Madrid, and was impressed by his intelligence and struggles against the Obiang regime. "Our whole friendship was built on my listening to his story, not business," Calil said after we had left Eronat in Paris and flown to Madrid to see Moto. "Sure, you could make money in Equatorial Guinea, and, sure, if Severo was there and the business was there I'd be interested, but that doesn't allow you to extrapolate and say, therefore, I arranged a coup to put him in power."

Calil also acknowledged knowing Simon Mann, but he insists he knew nothing about a coup; by his account, Mann was offering only to provide military protection for Moto so he could return to Equatorial Guinea. Obiang has brought suit against Calil over the coup in various countries, including Lebanon and Zimbabwe, and has never won a court victory. In Britain, a judge ruled that Obiang could not even bring a legal case for lack of evidence. "It would have been great fun," Calil told me. "He accused me of causing him mental trauma, and he would have been forced to come to court for a mental exam. He has tried every angle and opportunity, and lost each time. In the media I'm supposed to be the bad guy but Obiang treats his country as his kingdom and the oil like his private property." He added, "You had an African dictator and some mercenaries and a shady Arab. It makes for a great novel, but the part of it that wasn't a novel was tested in court and proven to be wrong. The press has reported a pack of lies."

Calil stayed at the Ritz Hotel in Madrid, and we met Moto and one of his daughters late one afternoon at the lobby bar, where a pianist played "New York, New York." Moto was dressed in a black jacket, a lavender shirt, and tasseled loafers; he pulled out typed press statements for my review from a faux leopard-skinned binder. The Spanish government had recently been threatening to force him to leave the country, and he seemed downcast and depressed, aware that any chance he had once had of ruling Equatorial Guinea was quickly and irreversibly slipping away. "For many years I had very good and important friends in Spain that helped me financially and politically, but the government has cut off all that help," he told me, as he drank a Coca-Cola with a slice of lemon. "Fortunately, God put Ely in my path. Every time I have asked Ely for support, he has responded."

But Moto denied he and Calil ever talked about a coup or that he discussed overthrowing Obiang during his conversations with Simon Mann. "I was told he [Mann] had great capacity in providing personal protection," he said.

"I presented my plan to him to return to Equatorial Guinea and my fear that Obiang would assassinate me. He assured me that he would be able to offer protection if I returned, but he never said anything about a coup d'état. We never discussed that."

At this point Calil interjected: "Yes, Severo was going in, and he needed to be accompanied ... But it was only to accompany him home; it was not to stage a coup. Simon Mann wouldn't even know how to take his own mother to the ball."

In recent years, the global energy business has changed in ways that have reduced somewhat the clout of the middleman. Following the expansion of antibribery laws, a number of companies and fixers have been tried for their illegal payoffs to foreign officials. In addition to the Halliburton case involving Jack Stanley and Jeffrey Tesler, the oil services company Baker Hughes paid a $33 million fine after admitting it had bribed officials in Angola, Russia, and other countries. Willbros Group, another oil services company, was found to have paid off numerous foreign officials to win overseas deals, in one case delivering $1 million in a suitcase. Such judgments have made companies more wary of fixers and more eager to find other means of securing political support. One especially popular technique has been to partner with a local company that is owned by a president, or oil minister, or some other top official that needs to be appeased.

Oil-rich states have grown a bit more sophisticated, too, further lessening the utility of middlemen. When the Soviet Union collapsed in the early 1990s, such newly formed oil producers as Kazakhstan and Azerbaijan had no experience whatsoever with international business. Russia was hardly better off, and so fixers like Calil and Eronat were able to get in early and serve as important oil exporters from the country. "Everyone was using everyone," Calil told me of that time. "The Russians were using you because they didn't have the capital or the knowledge. You were using the Russians because you needed a local partner. But then the Russians acquired the knowledge and the money, so they no longer need you anymore."

In West Africa, after decades of poverty, deficient education, and repressive rule, many governments were staffed entirely by untrained apparatchiks who had no idea how to interact in the business arena. But during the 2000s, year after year of ever-rising oil prices prompted many oil nations to become savvier about their resources and more inclined to deal with corporations directly.

Fixers remain a permanent presence in the oil markets, however, and for good reason. Even with prices dropping in the current slowdown, a worldwide scramble for oil is still under way, with the United States and China as the two major competitors. Companies are always looking for an advantage, and often the right fixer can be the means to gain it. "There's no way one company can act clean, especially if you're worrying about what the Chinese and Koreans are going to do," Edward Chow, the former Chevron executive, told me. "And to be fair, if you're working for a Chinese or Indian oil company, and you're trying to get into a country or region where the Americans or British or French have been forever, how do you think you're going to get in?" Furthermore, oil companies today tend to be capital-rich but opportunity-poor: They have plenty of money, but there are fewer fields and concessions available, and much of what's out there is controlled by national oil companies. So the stakes are higher and the desperation to get in is greater. "The fundamental drivers behind the use of fixers are so strong that it's hard to imagine the practice is going to go away," Chow said.

Calil agrees, in characteristically blunt terms. "There's no way to do business in the Third World without enriching government leaders," he told me. "You used to give a dictator a suitcase of dollars; now you give a tip on your stock shares, or buy a housing estate from his uncle or mother for ten times its worth." Because of this inevitability, Calil sees the West's strict antibribery laws as fundamentally misguided. "If you want to end corruption, you have to become the policeman of the world, and put in prison—in America—the Obiangs and Dos Santoses. But the businessman has no choice but to do what those guys want. He's between the devil and the deep blue sea. The Chinese are coming to Africa and promising 25 percent for concessions. So what do you do? Say the US government doesn't approve? The Chinese will give you the finger ... No one looks forward to paying bribes. It's no joke, and it's coming out of [the fixer's] pocket, not yours or Uncle Sam's. But if you have to do it, you have to do it."

Calil has oil interests still, but he has diversified into a broader range of industries. He spends more and more of his time "managing my investments," among them interests in the emerging field of carbon trading: buying the rights to pollute from cleaner businesses and selling them to dirtier ones. A firm he is involved with had struck deals in China and India, and Calil was traveling regularly to both nations on the company's behalf, hoping to establish business ties and build political support. It was an ironic turn indeed that Ely Calil, who grew so rich off the excesses of the carbon era, should now stand to profit still more from the long struggle to clean them up.

2

The Dictators: Teodorin Obiang

The owner of the estate at 3620 Sweetwater Mesa Road, which sits high above Malibu, California, called himself a prince, and he certainly lived like one. A long, tree-lined driveway runs from the estate's main gate past a motor court with fountains and down to a fifteen-thousand-square-foot mansion that has eight bathrooms and an equal number of fireplaces. The grounds overlook the Pacific Ocean, complete with a swimming pool, a tennis court, and a four-hole golf course, spill across a hilltop lot so expansive that the household staff use golf carts to move about the property. Past and present residents of the neighborhood, called Serra Retreat, include Mel Gibson, Britney Spears, and Sylvester Stallone.

With a short, stocky build, slicked-back hair, and Coke-bottle glasses, the prince hardly presents an image of royal elegance. But his wardrobe was picked from the racks of Versace, Gucci, and Dolce & Gabbana, and he spared no expense on himself, from the $30 million in cash he paid for the estate to vast sums for household furnishings: a $59,850 rug, a $58,000 home theater, $1,734.17 for a pair of wineglasses. When the prince departed or arrived at his home—usually in the backseat of a chauffeur-driven Rolls-Royce or one of his other several dozen cars—his employees were instructed to stand in a receiving line to greet him.

The prince, though, was a phony, a descendant of rulers but not of royals. His full name was Teodoro Nguema Obiang Mangue—Teodorin to friends—and he is the son of the dictator of the West African nation of Equatorial Guinea. A postage stamp of a country with a population of a mere 650,000 souls, Equatorial Guinea would be of little international consequence if it didn't have one thing: oil, and plenty of it. It is sub-Saharan Africa's third-largest producer, after Nigeria and Angola, and pumps more than three hundred thousand barrels per day. American energy firms have collectively invested several billion dollars over the past fifteen years in Equatorial Guinea, which exports more of its crude to the US market than any other country.

Equatorial Guinea's economy depends almost entirely on oil, which generated revenues in 2010 of well over $4 billion, giving it a per capita annual income of $37,900, on par with Belgium. "The oil has been for us like the manna that the Jews ate in the desert," Teodorin's father, President Teodoro Obiang Nguema Mbasogo, has said. It certainly has been for him. Obiang placed eighth on a 2006 list by *Forbes* of the world's richest leaders, with a personal fortune estimated at that time of $600 million.[1] His population hasn't fared so well. Nearly four fifths of Equatorial

Guinea's people live in abject poverty, and one in three dies before age forty.

Obiang's corruption is hardly unique among oil-rich dictators. French authorities uncovered thirty-nine properties in France and seventy French bank accounts held by the family of President Omar Bongo, who ruled Gabon for forty-one years until his death in 2009. (Soon thereafter, his son, Ali Bongo, took power.) Denis Sassou Nguesso, the leader of Congo-Brazzaville, bought a variety of French properties with tens of millions of dollars in oil revenues funneled out of his country. "All the leaders of the world have castles and palaces in France, whether they are from the Gulf, Europe, or Africa," Sassou Nguesso said several years ago by way of explanation. In Central Asia, fantastically rich new oil-endowed ruling families have exploited energy wealth with great panache, too, from throwing birthday parties featuring Elton John to doling out luxury villas to friends and family.

But the scale of his regime's looting appears to be approaching the sort of baroque levels reached before by historic crooks like Zairian dictator Mobutu Sese Seko, America's closest friend in Africa during the Cold War, and Nigerian general Sani Abacha, who moved several billion dollars into Swiss accounts. "There are many reported instances where the African state has degenerated to a kleptocracy, characterized by the intense personalization of authority and the voraciousness of a small state elite and their core constituents," writes Geoffrey Wood, a professor now at Warwick Business School.

The Equatoguinean state, however, is relatively distinct both on account of the extreme personalization of authority and the relationship between the government and a range of supporting legal, quasi-legal and criminal enterprises. Indeed, it is one of the few African countries that can be correctly classified as a criminal state.

Wood penned those lines in 2004; since then, corruption and criminalization have only worsened. Indeed, Equatorial Guinea is effectively a mafia state in which power and wealth are tightly controlled by a brutal gang family and a small number of cronies and enforcers. Gabriel Obiang, another of the president's sons, is second in command of, but effectively runs, the ministry of mines and energy, which oversees the oil sector. Though he spent long stretches outside of his home country, Teodorin holds the ministry of forestry and environment, which oversees the timber trade, the nation's only other notable export. The president's wife, Constancia, is one of the most powerful people in the country, with economic stakes that range from real estate to construction. One of her brothers runs the state oil company while another is a former ambassador to the US and to Brazil, one of the clan's favorite playgrounds to spend its ill-gotten loot. The president's direct relatives hold the top positions at key state treasury agencies and across the national security establishment.

The clan's ostentatious thievery has attracted the attention of investigators in multiple countries and three continents. A Spanish court is investigating a complaint charging that President Obiang and ten relatives and associates used $26.5 million in laundered money to buy houses and chalets in

Madrid and the Canary Islands. In France, a police corruption inquiry uncovered tens of millions of dollars' worth of assets belonging to the Obiang gang, including $6.3 million worth of luxury cars owned by Teodorin and a mansion on Avenue Foch, just off the Champs-Élysées, worth as much as $200 million. In October 2012 police raided the mansion and, according to a report in the *Telegraph*, carted off

> two full lorry loads of belongings, including a Rodin statue, 10 Fabergé eggs, 300 bottles of Chateau Petrus wine worth 2.1 million euros and 18.5 million euros worth of art works bought from the 2009 sale of Yves Saint Laurent's private collection.

The story said Teodorin's estate included "a disco, cinema, steam baths, sauna, hair salon, gold- and jewel-encrusted taps, lift, and pink marble dining room with coral pillars and 20-yard glass table, all overlooking the Arc de Triomphe." Soon afterward the French government issued an international arrest warrant for Teodorin.

In October 2011, the US government filed a civil asset forfeiture complaint seeking to take possession of tens of millions of dollars in assets held by Teodorin Obiang. The complaint, filed by the Justice Department and the Department of Homeland Security's Immigration and Customs Enforcement (ICE) arm, said that high officials in the Obiang regime had "gained enormous wealth" through methods that included "extortion and misappropriation, theft, and embezzlement of public funds." It specifically alleged that Teodorin funneled more than $100 million into the United States through shell companies to buy his

Malibu estate, plane, and Michael Jackson memorabilia. Investigators said that Teodorin supplemented his modest ministerial salary of about $6,800 per month—a figure they described, with some understatement, as being "inconsistent" with his level of spending—with a "revolutionary tax" on timber, which he demanded international logging firms pay to a forestry company he owned.

Obiang Sr. seized power in a 1979 coup and has made apparent his intent to hand over power to a chosen successor. He has sired an unknown number of children with multiple women, but Teodorin is his clear favorite and is being groomed to take over. That's a scary prospect both for the long-suffering citizens of his country and for US foreign policy. As a former US intelligence official familiar with Teodorin put it to me, "He's an unstable, reckless idiot." He's also fantastically corrupt. US investigators have documented how he runs the agriculture and forestry ministry like a business—earning him the nickname of the "Minister of Chopping Down Trees"—and operates several logging companies alongside the agency meant to regulate them.

Teodorin's vast wealth has fueled a lavish and debauched lifestyle, which is detailed in a series of civil lawsuits filed against him by more than a dozen former employees at his Malibu estate. They claim they were cheated out of salaries, overtime wages, and work-related expenses for items ranging from gasoline to toilet paper, while being forced to support a tawdry setup straight out of the movie *The Hangover*. There were escort service girls, drug binges, Playboy bunnies, and even a tiger. "I never witnessed him perform anything that looked like work," read a legal filing on behalf of Dragan Deletic, one of Teodorin's former drivers. "His days consisted entirely of sleeping, shopping and partying."

Kevin Fisher, a Los Angeles lawyer for Teodorin, dismissed the employees' charges as "salacious," "extreme," and "unverified." Yet after years of wrangling, Teodorin ended up settling most of the cases. The employees signed agreements that prevent them from speaking about Teodorin, but prior to that I read the case filings and interviewed a number of the plaintiffs and their attorney, Jim McDermott.

The 2011 asset forfeiture complaint marks a big step forward, but by the time it was filed—more than four years after the investigation began—Teodorin had transferred most of his assets out of the United States, beyond the reach of law enforcement. It would have been a simple matter to put a halt to his excesses years earlier. In 2004, President George W. Bush issued Proclamation 7750, which bars corrupt foreign officials from receiving US visas. Barack Obama, Bush's successor, pledged that his administration would vigorously enforce 7750, saying, "No country is going to create wealth if its leaders exploit the economy to enrich themselves. We have a responsibility to support those who act responsibly and to isolate those who don't."[2]

Yet both the Bush and Obama administrations dallied for years while Teodorin flew in and out of the country unmolested and used the state of California as his personal shopping mall. And while Obama has been mildly cooler than Bush toward the government of Equatorial

Guinea, he has said little publicly about its awful record of corruption and human rights violations and failed to impose sanctions against the state Teodorin is set to inherit. Why? It certainly appears to be the familiar story of the US government being unwilling to offend an important oil partner—the same coddling that has produced such stellar results in the past with Saudi Arabia and other energy-rich, democracy-poor Middle East allies. Or as McDermott, the plaintiffs' attorney, put it, "In our system of international politics, there's a lot of ass-kissing, especially if there's oil involved."

Just fifteen years ago, Equatorial Guinea was of little geopolitical interest to any nation other than its direct neighbors. Roughly the size of Maryland—the country is composed of a few islands and a square of land on the continent wedged between Gabon and Cameroon—it was one of the most isolated countries in the world, with much of the population engaged in subsistence farming of rice, yams, and bananas.

The political picture was equally grim. Francisco Macías Nguema, a West African version of Idi Amin, took power upon its independence in 1968. He soon banned opposition parties and appointed himself "president for life"—along with a number of other self-decreed titles that included the "implacable apostle of freedom" and "the sole miracle of Equatorial Guinea." Macías sought to eliminate all of his enemies, both real and imagined, holding mass executions at the country's major soccer stadium and crucifying (literally) political prisoners.

In 1979 the sole miracle was overthrown and subsequently executed by Obiang, his nephew. Obiang was no reformer. As head of the National Guard and later commander of the armed forces, he played a major role in carrying out the terrible repression of the Macías years, and was already skilled in the art of dictatorship after running Black Beach prison, a notorious torture chamber for political prisoners. "He presided over the killings of thousands of people," says John Bennett, a former American ambassador to Equatorial Guinea. "He was the chief executioner."

Over the past three decades, Obiang has been "elected" three times, most recently in 2009, when he won 95.4 percent of the vote (a record low; he peaked with 97.85 percent in 1996). The State Department's 2011 global report on human rights in Equatorial Guinea says security forces "acted independently of civilian control" and were guilty of a long list of abuses, including unlawful killings, summary executions, torture, arbitrary arrest, and incommunicado detention. There is no independent radio or television in Equatorial Guinea. A few years ago an announcer on a state-owned radio station declared that President Obiang was "in permanent contact with the Almighty" and has the authority to "kill without anyone calling him to account."

For years US officials looked upon the country as a laughingstock. Frank Ruddy, US ambassador to Equatorial Guinea during the Reagan years, tells the story of one of Obiang's top aides, who was fortunate to benefit from diplomatic immunity, being stopped at New York's JFK airport with a suitcase full of marijuana. The police had little trouble making the bust: The aide's bag had a hole in the side, and he was trailing pot as he strolled through the terminal. (More seriously, there have been numerous credible allegations of international drug trafficking by regime members.)

There's also a story that was widely circulated in CIA circles about how two of Obiang's intelligence operatives came to Washington in the mid-1980s to meet top agency officials. The Equatoguinean went shopping at a suburban Virginia mall beforehand and came to the meeting dressed in identical outfits: black business suits and electric Nike sneakers.

US officials paid little interest to the country beyond periodically criticizing its poor record on political rights and democracy. Then, in 1994, John Bennett, the US ambassador based in Malabo at the time, was threatened with death after he called for improved human rights conditions. "You will go to America as a corpse," he was warned in a message thrown from the window of a vehicle passing his residence—a vehicle that eyewitnesses said was driven by a government official. Two years later the Clinton administration shut down the American embassy in Malabo.

The move was barely noted and seemed of little concern. The country was a destitute pariah and seemed destined to fade into obscurity. But just a few weeks after the embassy closed its doors, US companies found significant petroleum reserves off the coast of Equatorial Guinea. Over the next few years firms such as ExxonMobil and Chevron, as well as independents such as Ocean Energy, Vanco, and Triton (all three later sold their stakes), collectively invested billions of dollars in Equatorial Guinea.

As US economic interests grew, a slow political shift in Washington–Malabo relations emerged. In June 2000, with American oil company executives starting to call Equatorial Guinea the "Kuwait of Africa," the Overseas Private Investment Corporation, a US government agency, approved $173 million in loan guarantees to build an American-owned methanol plant there, at the time its largest program ever in sub-Saharan Africa. Later that year, Louisiana congressman William Jefferson led the first-ever congressional delegation to Equatorial Guinea, where he was greeted effusively by the government and given a key to the city of Malabo.[3]

A particularly marked improvement in relations occurred after George W. Bush took office in 2001. It surely helped Obiang's cause that the companies active in Equatorial Guinea had close ties to the Bush administration and lobbied strongly on his behalf: In addition to well-known political powerhouses such as ExxonMobil and Chevron, there was Dallas-based Triton, whose chairman, Tom Hicks, made George W. Bush a millionaire fifteen times over when he bought the Texas Rangers in 1998, and whose leveraged buyout firm, Hicks Muse, was one of Bush's largest career campaign financial patrons.[4]

In 2001, American oil companies retained lobbyist K. Riva Levinson to advocate for the reopening of the US Embassy in Malabo.[5] In a memo to the Bush administration that argued the case, Levinson said, "Most of the oil and gas concessions awarded in Equatorial Guinea to date have been awarded to US firms. This is in stark contrast to neighboring countries in the region, where the United States has consistently lost out to ... [European] competitors."

In June of the next year Levinson helped arrange meetings for government officials at the Department of Energy. Two months later the two countries signed a memorandum of understanding that aimed to expand the US presence in Equatorial Guinea's oil and gas sector.

In addition to direct lobbying, Obiang found help buffing his regime's image from Bruce McColm, a former head of Freedom House who founded the Institute for Democratic Strategies (IDS), a Virginia-based nonprofit with a stated mission of "strengthening democratic institutions." Virtually all of McColm's funding came from oil companies or the Obiang government, and he tireless championed his patrons' cause.

In 2000 McColm sent a team of observers to monitor Equatorial Guinea's municipal elections, which it reported to be basically free and fair. "Electoral officials should be recognized for discharging their responsibilities in an effective and transparent manner," said an IDS press release at the time. "Observers generally felt that the positives of this election far outweighed the negatives." This was in marked contrast to a UN report that said the electoral campaign "was characterized by the omnipresence of the [ruling] party, voting in public, and the intimidating presence of the armed forces."

The oil companies also worked through the Corporate Council on Africa, which represents companies with investments on the continent. In 2002, it sponsored a private luncheon for Obiang, who was visiting Washington with a small entourage. The event was held in the chandeliered dining room of downtown Washington's Army-Navy Club, and each of the roughly fifty guests in attendance received a biography of Obiang prepared by McColm's IDS that describes him as the country's "first democratically elected president" and a man who has "embarked on the total physical reconstruction of his country and the improvement of the welfare of all its citizens."

Sporting gold-rimmed glasses and dressed in a blue suit with American and Equatoguinean flag pins on the lapels, Obiang sat at the head table, where he was dwarfed by oilmen and State Department officials. During a lunch of fish stuffed with crabmeat and a custard tart with raspberry syrup, a procession of five corporate executives sought to outdo each other in heaping praise on Obiang and his nation. "It will be the Kuwait of Africa," gushed one of the speakers, Gene Van Dyke of Vanco. "It's a fabulous country."

When it came time for him to speak, the guest of honor congratulated the American people for the great faith they displayed in the aftermath of September 11 and said that he too knew the importance of faith. "There was a time when we thought we didn't have oil," he said. "There was oil to the north, oil to the south, but none here. But I had faith— faith that Equatorial Guinea had oil."

Political turmoil in the Middle East indirectly aided the oil industry's overtures on Obiang's behalf, as did Africa's broader role as a growing oil exporter to the US. By 2000, the United States was already buying 15 percent of its oil imports from Africa, with Nigeria and Angola the two biggest individual suppliers and Equatorial Guinea poised to grow quickly. "Sub-Saharan Africa is an area of US vital interest, and is also of increasing strategic importance to the United States as it applies to American energy security needs," Paul Michael Wihbey, then of the Institute for Advanced Strategic and Political Studies, told a congressional subcommittee in March of 2000.[6] The September 11 attacks the following year led national security planners to call for greater diversification of imports away from the Middle East, especially toward non-OPEC suppliers in Africa and Central Asia.

This was also a theme emphasized by the industry itself in seeking to build support for new alliances with dodgy regimes like Equatorial Guinea. "This is one of the hottest spots in the world right now," Jim Musselman, the head of Triton Energy, told me when I met him in Malabo in 2002. He was comfortably ensconced in one of the many government villas that the the government, already flush with oil revenues, had built for visiting foreign dignitaries and businessmen.

An affable, balding man who wore a blue dress shirt and cowboy boots embossed with his initials, Musselman described himself as "an unabashed fan" of Equatorial Guinea. "There is plenty of instability in the world, and the more diverse supplies of oil we have, the better off things are," he told me. "Knock on wood, this country is stable and the president is sincerely trying to improve things. It's not going to turn into suburban Washington, but it could be a model for this part of the world."

In 2003, the oil industry and Obiang won their goal: The embassy in Malabo reopened—in a building owned by the minister of national security who is both a relative of Obiang's and an accused torturer. Since then the US government has rarely criticized the Obiang regime other than for in the pro forma annual State Department human rights reports and milquetoast appeals for better behavior. In April 2006, then secretary of state Condoleezza Rice met with Obiang in Washington and called him a "good friend" of the United States. Three years later, a smiling President Obama posed for a photo with Obiang during a reception at the Metropolitan Museum of Art in New York, marking a minor PR coup for the regime. (This was just two months after Obiang had again won reelection via sham balloting.) "With the increased US investment presence, relations between the US and the Government of Equatorial Guinea have been characterized as positive and constructive," the State Department says of ties between the two countries.

In the mid-1990s, President Obiang opened accounts at Riggs Bank in Washington DC. He claimed in documents filed with the bank that cocoa farming was the source of wealth. Riggs didn't bother checking that assertion carefully, though it was supposed to do serious due diligence before opening an account for a politically exposed person, the term for a foreign national who holds a senior office.

In fact, there is no known record of Obiang having been a farmer or owning much land or wealth before he seized power. He simply swiped prime state cocoa farms—which

Macías had nationalized after stealing them from Spanish landholders who fled following independence—and appropriated them for himself and his cronies.

In his book *Tropical Gangsters*, Robert Klitgaard—who lived in Equatorial Guinea in the 1980s as a World Bank official charged with reforming the economy—described a confidential trip report written by two members of an English cocoa firm that did extensive business in the country:

> The document was amazing in frankness and detail. It referred to price fixing and other scams between exporters and importers, such as pretending that so much cocoa of such-and-such quality was shipped when actually the quality and quantity were much higher. It described bribes to several Equatoguinean ministers. Most remarkably, it detailed the company's corrupt deals with President Obiang and his lawyer. Reading the document was like a kick in the gut. Even though I had written a book about Third World corruption, seldom had I seen such blatant, almost casual evidence of graft.

Klitgaard said that after the World Bank had approved a big cocoa project in late 1983, "top government officials had foreseen a gold mine." Knowing that the bank would be giving credit to those with cocoa farms, they all rushed out—with a helping hand from the president—to obtain land. And so in 1984 the choicest cocoa farms were simply taken over by government ministers. Klitgaard wrote:

> The Prime Minister had a beauty near Luba, and the President himself seized nearly four thousand acres near the Malabo airport.

These new "farmers" went to [state banks] and demanded loans, and got them. Often the money they received was squandered on cars and video recorders, not on lime and copper sulfate for the cocoa trees. Inevitably, yields plummeted; when the ministers couldn't repay their loans they simply defaulted.

Former ambassador Bennett told me that during his time in the country Obiang and family members "took a cut" on every import into and export out of the port, which the president ran as a private commercial enterprise. Still, during the early years of his rule, the national economy simply didn't generate enough revenue to allow the Obiang clan to reach the big leagues of corruption.

The situation began to change in the early 1990s when Walter International, an independent Texas-based firm, began operating a small natural gas field in the country. Its entry into Equatorial Guinea was negotiated by then US ambassador Chester Norris, who maintained a friendly relationship with the Obiang regime. After retiring in 1991 he took a job as the personal representative of Walter International's president. The Obiang government was so fond of Norris that it named a street for him in an exclusive suburb for foreign oil executives.

By the early 2000s, oil production was beginning to ramp up, and Equatorial Guinea had hundreds of millions of dollars, all of it deposited by American oil companies in an account at Riggs. Though a state account, it was effectively controlled by President Obiang. Riggs also opened up dozens of personal accounts for the president and his relatives, some of them offshore. These include a money

market account that was set up for the president in the
name of a Bahamas-registered corporation that received
deposits of $11.5 million in cash between 2000 and 2002.
Some of the deposits into the Riggs accounts were made
by Equatoguinean officials walking in with as much as $1
million in shrink-wrapped bills. "Riggs ... turned a blind
eye to evidence suggesting the bank was handling the
proceeds of foreign corruption, and allowed numerous
suspicious transactions to take place without notifying law
enforcement," concluded a 2004 Senate investigation.[7]

Riggs assigned senior vice president Simon Kareri to the
Obiang family as its private banker. As part of his duties,
Kareri (now deceased) in 2000 assisted Obiang's brother,
Armengol Ondo Nguema, in buying a Virginia townhouse
for $349,000 in cash. (Nguema still owns the townhouse,
which is currently assessed at $608,000.) A State Department
report on human rights violations in Equatorial Guinea the
previous year said that Ondo Nguema, who at the time
headed the country's security apparatus, had directed his
men to urinate on prisoners and slice their ears with knives
and smear oil over their naked bodies to attract stinging
ants. "Mr. Armengol Ondo Nguema is a valued customer
of Riggs Bank," Kareri wrote to the seller's agent in the
townhouse deal, in a letter that guaranteed that the security
chieftain had sufficient funds to pay for the property. After
he bought it, Riggs set up an account to pay the bills and
taxes for his house. His four children, who attended schools
in Virginia, lived at the property.

The Obiangs were demanding clients. "Teodorin called
Simon all the time to say pay this or pay that," said a source

who knew Kareri well. "Once he was on a cruise ship with his latest girlfriend and called and said, 'I'm tired of this bitch, send a helicopter and get her'."

One Riggs document uncovered by the Senate identified a giant holding company owned by the president called Abayak, whose interests included real estate, cement, construction, oil and gas, and banking. The company was made a partner in various business projects set up by American energy firms and was "a significant earner of income for the president," the document said.

Journalist Peter Maass asked a logical question when reporting a story for *Mother Jones* magazine: "What did Abayak offer its American partners other than the name and blessing of the president?" To find out he visited Abayak's seven-story building, which he described as the biggest building in the country. When Maass got there he discovered that Abayak was no bustling enterprise but operated out of two rooms on the top floor. "If these were Abayak's headquarters, they seemed unfathomably modest for a firm that had been selected as a partner by the largest oil companies in the world," he wrote. A source told him that Abayak "functioned mainly as a vehicle through which payments were made in exchange for the president's approval of business projects."

The 2004 Senate report found that American oil companies were deeply in bed with the Obiang clan. Both ExxonMobil and Amerada Hess hired Sonavi, a private security firm headed by Ondo Nguema, the torturer. ExxonMobil leased land from Abayak, and Marathon Oil bought 625 acres of land from the president's company.

Amerada Hess paid government officials and their relatives more than $2 million to lease properties in Equatorial Guinea, of which about one-quarter went to a fourteen-year-old boy, a relative of Obiang's.

Even worse were sweetheart business deals the oil companies handed to the dictator. ExxonMobil gave President Obiang a 15 percent stake in an oil trading business for a mere $2,300. Within six years his holding had increased in value by 280 times. Abayak received a combined stake, worth as much as $29 million, in two joint ventures that Marathon inherited when it bought CMS Energy's Equatorial Guinea holdings in 2002. Obiang's holding company put no money down for its initial shares and received more than $1 million in dividend payments from the two ventures between 2002 and 2003 alone.[8]

To any lucid observer the oil companies had found creative if obvious means of bribing Obiang. But while the US government opened a Foreign Corrupt Practices Act investigation of five major companies doing business in Equatorial Guinea, it never brought charges against any of them.

The Senate report proved to be highly embarrassing to Equatorial Guinea and its American friends. At a hearing to which oil company executives were called to testify about the report, Senator Carl Levin told them, "I don't see any fundamental difference between dealing with an Obiang and dealing with a Saddam Hussein."

None of this altered the behavior of the Obiang regime. As more and more oil revenues flowed into the state treasury, the clan designed and refined a modus operandi that ensured that most of the money ended up directly in its pockets. For example, the president or his family is reliably reported to demand a stake in virtually any significant foreign investment project, generally through one of the corporate vehicles they control. "Obiang's approval always incurs an equity holding in whatever company comes in," a businessman who lived in Equatorial Guinea for ten years explained. "Say I bring company X to Equatorial Guinea and we get a road contract. We have to open a local operating company, called, say, XCO-EG. Then Abayak or another Obiang company takes a stake in that company."

This person said that it was understood by all parties that "the president had to be a shareholder" in any large investment, and that there was not "a single major operation that Obiang is not involved in."

Teodorin has freely admitted that as a cabinet minister he takes a significant cut of government contracts, an arrangement that is another core component of the clan MO. In a sworn affidavit filed with a court in South Africa, he stated:

Cabinet Ministers and public servants in Equatorial Guinea are by law allowed to own companies that, in consortium with a foreign company, can bid for government Contracts and should the company be successful, then what percentage of the total cost of the Contract the company gets, will depend on the terms negotiated between the parties. But, in any event, it means that a cabinet minister ends up with a sizeable part of the Contract price in his bank account.

For the Obiang regime, the state budget is essentially a funnel to move money into the hands of clan members, as seen in federal construction contracts. Cabinet officials who own private companies "divert government funds for their personal use by submitting inflated bids for government contracts," the Justice Department reported. "Those companies are able to charge ... fees that bear little, if any, rational relationship to the actual economic value of the services or products tendered." Markups on such deals ranged as high as 500 percent.

Teodorin was appointed as minister in 1998, at the ripe old age of thirty. Five years later, his father awarded him a twenty-year concession to harvest timber from twenty-five thousand hectares of rain forest. (A Malaysian company did the actual logging.) The following year, Teodorin created a forestry company called Sofona, to which his father granted a five-year concession to harvest timber from an additional eleven thousand hectares. He soon created a second forestry company called Somagui Forestal, with this entire arrangment being roughly equivalent to the US defense secretary owning Lockheed Martin and Boeing.

Teodorin has claimed that his current wealth does not stem from corrupt activities but accrues from the profitable logging companies he operates in Equatorial Guinea. However, a local timber firm operator told the Justice Department that his companies "had no function other than to open bank accounts and receive illegal payments."

Teodorin's stewardship of his ministry has been disastrous for the country, both financially and environmentally. Logging in Equatorial Guinea has declined in recent years, which the government attributes to its conservation efforts. More impartial observers say this decline stems from the fact that there are simply not that many trees left: Teodorin's ministry has facilitated the rapid depletion of forest resources in the country.

The Justice Department alleges that companies that bribed Teodorin—the precise sums required were "calculated by technicians" on his staff—could log wherever they liked, including in reserves allegedly protected under the country's laws. Companies that refused to pay bribes got kicked out of the country and had their property and equipment stolen.

Teodorin told one senior executive of a foreign firm that he would "suffer" because of his refusal to make payoffs, according to the Justice Department. The unnamed executive was later arrested and jailed. When he was freed he left the country upon the advice of "an E.G. national familiar with [Teodorin]" who told him he should flee immediately "if he did not want his children in Europe to become orphans."

According to a foreign timber executive who lived in Equatorial Guinea in the 1990s, Teodorin had acquired a notorious reputation among the country's logging companies even before officially taking over as minister. He quickly earned the nickname "El Niño" from foreign timber executives, due to the storms that he would kick up when he flew back to Equatorial Guinea from lengthy vacations abroad. "He would call emergency meetings of all the logging company heads in which he would announce some new tax on logging operations," the source said.

Teodorin slapped an extra "tax"—payable directly to him—on wood harvested from Equatorial Guinea. "Each company paid a royalty to the state treasury for each cubic meter of log shipped," this person said. "This might be a hundred dollars per cubic meter. Above that, each company also had to pay an amount per cubic meter directly to Teodorin."

The head of one Asia-based logging firm complained to this source that "keeping Teodorin happy" was costing serious amounts of money. Teodorin would allegedly contact the firm from Paris or the United States "and demand they immediately wire him fifty or a hundred thousand dollars." A Spanish logging firm that had long operated in Equatorial Guinea got so fed up with paying bribes that it sold out. Even then the buyer of its concession was required to pay several million dollars to Teodorin to approve the transfer.

Teodorin maintains revenues collected by the forestry ministry at a private commercial bank in an account over which he has sole signatory power and exclusive control. No other government official, including the Parliament or ministry of finance, "possesses the authority or ability to supervise, regulate or inspect how funds in the account are used," the Justice Department complaint says.

The Obiang clan's extravagances are all the more galling because Equatorial Guinea's natural resource wealth has led to few improvements for the country's people. In fact, numerous social welfare indicators have gotten worse, not better, since oil money started flowing in. The infant mortality rate climbed from 103 per 1,000 live births in 1990 to 124 in 2007 while the under-five mortality rate climbed during the same period from 170 to 206 per 1,000 births. The proportion of one-year-old children immunized against measles declined from 88 percent in 1990 to 51 percent in 2007. Net enrollment in primary education fell from 96.7 percent in 1991 to 69.4 percent in 2007.

And yet even money specifically earmarked for social programs has been stolen. The Justice Department complaint says:

> The Inner Circle routinely demands that companies operating in E.G. contribute money to what are disguised as public service campaigns [to build housing and other social programs. However] the contributions are not used for their alleged purpose, but instead are largely taken by members of the Inner Circle ... for their personal benefit.

As recently as July 2011, Teodorin raised funds from foreign companies for a program to improve housing for the poor by changing palm roofs to zinc tile roofs. Coincidentally, he

> possesses a substantial financial interest in the company that is responsible for distributing and supplying these zinc tiles ... [and] donor contributions are not used for their alleged purpose, but instead are largely misappropriated by [Teodorin] for his personal benefit.

*   *   *

The Obiang MO has allowed for a staggering accumulation of wealth by the ruling family and party members. The president owns multiple homes around the world, including two mansions in Potomac, Maryland, which he bought for about $4 million in cash in 2000 and two properties in Las Palmas in the Canary Islands.

In 2011, Obiang added to his real estate collection by buying a $10 million beachfront apartment in Rio de Janeiro. That same year he attended the city's famous Carnival celebration. According to an account in the local press, Obiang rented two floors at the Caesar Park Hotel in Ipanema and put up fifty guests. He also reportedly rented a double luxury suite to watch Rio's samba schools parade during the celebration. The suite was covered in red silk and featured a giant portrait of the president. He and his wife watched the parade on a white leather couch while serving guests champagne in crystal glasses.

First Lady Constancia, who has financial interests in everything from construction to oil to forestry, is also a big spender. Back in 2001 Kareri of Riggs Bank raised the daily limit on her debit card to ten thousand dollars to accommodate her shopping plans when visiting the US. "The twenty-five-hundred-dollar limit is insufficient for her needs," the banker wrote in a memo.

When it comes to Obiang family sleaze and corruption, though, Teodorin is indisputably Exhibit A. If by the standards of *The Godfather* films, President Obiang is Don Corleone, Teodorin is a combination of the brutal, violent Sonny and the drunken, skirt-chasing Fredo.

Despite his modest ministerial salary, the Justice

Department found that Teodorin "spent more than $300 million acquiring assets and property on four continents between 2000 and 2011—North America, South America, Europe and Africa." His holdings included his not only his Malibu and Paris estates and a $15 million property in São Paulo but millions of dollars worth of wine and paintings by Degas, Renoir, and Gauguin.

Perhaps his worst excesses took place in the Los Angeles area, where he's been a regular since 1991, when at the age of twenty-three he arrived at Pepperdine University in Malibu to attend an English as a Second Language course. I visited Pepperdine—home of the Waves and featuring the Sandbar Student Lounge and the Oasis Snack Bar—in the summer of 2011. Students in shorts and flip-flops strolled among palm trees and manicured lawns. They threw Frisbees across a small field, worked on their tennis games, and swam between orange and blue lane dividers, the school colors, at one of the campus pools.

Pepperdine's relaxed atmosphere must have been the ideal setting for young Teodorin. Walter International, the Texas firm that was the first to gain a stake in Equatorial Guinea's offshore fields, financed Teodorin's studies. Walter also agreed to pick up his living expenses, which proved to be a costly mistake. Teodorin's tuition for the nondegree course was a mere thirty-four hundred dollars, including boarding at Pepperdine. However, Teodorin deemed campus dormitories unsuitable and shuttled between two off-campus residences: a home he rented in Malibu and a suite at the Beverly Wilshire Hotel. He rarely attended class, instead spending his days shopping in Beverly Hills.

On the few occasions when he did come to campus he'd arrive in sports cars or limousines. Elisa Wax, director of the ESL course during that time, recalled Teodorin arriving at campus "He was there to party."

Wax received a steady stream of phone calls from the hotel, as well as from shops in Beverly Hills, trying to track down Teodorin to settle outstanding bills. She would direct these calls to a representative at Walter International. The woman assigned by Walter to handle these complaints was "pulling out her hair," Wax said. "There were people trying to locate him from all directions."

Teodorin dropped out of the program after five months; Walter International's tab for his expenses during that brief stay came to about fifty thousand dollars, according to former ambassador Bennett.

Teodorin traveled the world in subsequent years but returned frequently to the Los Angeles area. In 2001, he bought a $6.5 million home on Antelo Road in Bel Air, across from actress Farrah Fawcett. He never moved in, however, lamenting to a real estate agent that in retrospect the house was too contemporary for his taste.

Teodorin dreamed of being a hip-hop mogul, and for a time owned and operated a label whose name was derived from his initials: TNO Entertainment. TNO's most significant project appears to have been a flop titled *No Better Than This* by Won-G—a fitting collaboration given that the rapper, whose real name is Wondge Bruny, has described his father as a former military official under "Baby Doc" Duvalier, the Haitian dictator deposed in 1986. (The CD included a song called "I Love TNO.")

Teodorin continued to burn through cash during these years. He lived for a time at a Paris hotel off the Champs-Elysées; a French TV crew captured him on a shopping spree during which, it reported, he bought more than thirty suits in a single day. In 2004 he bought two estates worth a combined $7 million in Cape Town. But he and his family generally stayed off the radar screen in the United States until the Riggs scandal broke in 2004 and it became apparent just how much state revenue the family was siphoning off into its private bank accounts.

The following year Teodorin sought to open an account at Pacific Mercantile Bank, which utilized an internal system to rate the risk of doing business with new clients. A rating below nine suggested low or moderate risk, while a rating of nine or above constituted high risk. Teodorin was evaluated twice, coming in with scores of twenty-five and thirty-four. Pacific Mercantile took his money anyway, but many banks didn't want to touch Teodorin's cash.

Lesser kleptocrats might have turned tail and fled, but not Teodorin. To ensure adequate cash flow, he employed Michael Berger, a small-fry bankruptcy lawyer, and George Nagler, an accountant, to set up shell companies and associated bank accounts that he controlled but in which his name was hidden. The companies did no business but were merely vehicles for him to receive and spend funds wired from abroad.

E-mails obtained by the Senate revealed Berger to be an egregious sycophant. Teodorin hosted an annual party at his estate that he called the Nguema Summer Bash, which

Berger attended in 2007. In an e-mail to Teodorin the next day the attorney wrote:

> Thank you very much for inviting me to your party and for being so nice to me. The food was great, the drinks were better than great, the house, the view, the DJ, the white tiger were all SO COOL!

The following month Teodorin arranged for Berger to attend the Kandy Halloween Bash at the Playboy Mansion, which advertised "Body-Painted Models," "Go-Go Dancers," and "1,000 hand-picked Kandy Girls in the sexiest costumes." This prompted another fawning e-mail from Berger to Teodorin.

> I had an awesome time. I met many beautiful women, and I have the photos, e-mail addresses and phone numbers to prove it. If the word gets out that you are looking for a bride, women all over the world will go even more crazy for you.

He attached a photo of himself with several Kandy Girls, and wrote:

> Here's a sample of what your future may hold.[9]

In 2006, Teodorin used one of his shell companies, Sweetwater Malibu LLC, to purchase the Malibu estate. It is among the largest homes in Serra Retreat, a private neighborhood in which guards are posted round-the-clock at two entrances to keep out celebrity watchers and other uninvited visitors. I arranged to get a visitor's pass by contacting a real estate broker and feigning interest as a potential buyer of a home for sale not far from Teodorin's, and was waved through the main checkpoint. The road was lined with eucalyptus, palms, cactus, and bushes bursting with yellow and pink flowers, and climbed steeply up the hillside after passing Cross Creek Lane ("No one but celebrities lives there," a local realtor who accompanied me said). There were no residents along the road, but we passed numerous work crews doing landscaping work along the route. I drove just past Teodorin's house, which sits behind a high wall lined with security cameras, and parked along the roadside. His mansion was barely visible from the road, but the view of the Pacific was spectacular. The house sits directly above the Malibu pier, and the ocean was filled with swimmers and surfers. Anchored a few hundred feet offshore was a submarine-shaped super-yacht owned by Russian billionaire Andrey Melnichenko, which had turned up a few days earlier and been the talk of Malibu. I could see Santa Monica through the haze and, farther out, a strip of land called the Queen's Necklace, the farthest point south on the Palos Verdes Peninsula.

Benito Giacalone, one of Teodorin's former drivers, is a tall, handsome man with a neatly trimmed goatee. He met me at a Starbucks in Beverly Hills, where he recounted his hiring in early 2009. "An employment agency called and told me that there was an African prince who needed a driver," said Giacalone, who wore a gray pinstriped suit, with a pair of sunglasses hooked through the top button of a white shirt. "That seemed strange; I've worked with

Middle Eastern royalty, and I was pretty sure there weren't many princes from Africa."

He drove to the mansion, where about ten other applicants had arrived before him and were queued up outside the main gate. Some eight hours later, by which time most of the candidates had tired of waiting and left, Sula Symonds—a model and aspiring actress who doubled as Teodorin's estate manager and periodic girlfriend—interviewed Giacalone. He was called the following day and told to come to work immediately; his first assignment was to drive Teodorin to the airport in Van Nuys, where his jet was waiting to fly him to Equatorial Guinea. It was pouring rain, and as Giacalone waited for Teodorin at the wheel of a Maybach, one of dozens of sports cars owned by his new boss, he opened the glove box and saw the name on the registration. "I still didn't know who he was until then, only that he was supposed to be a prince," he said. "I did a Google search on my BlackBerry and found out who he really was. I knew I was in for a ride, but I really needed the job."

When it came to spending habits, Teodorin wasn't to be outdone by his Hollywood-star neighbors. He owned at least three dozen luxury cars, including seven Ferraris, five Bentleys, four Rolls-Royces, two Lamborghinis, two Mercedes-Benzes, two Porsches, two Maybachs, and an Aston Martin, with a combined insured value of around $10 million, according to the Senate investigation. There were far too many cars to keep at the estate, so Teodorin rented storage space in the garage of the Petersen Automotive Museum on Wilshire Boulevard and had his drivers fetch the one he wanted for an outing, a choice that sometimes depended on his attire. "I'm wearing blue shoes, so get me the blue Rolls today," he once told Giacalone.

His favorite was a Bugatti Veyron, a car that can reach speeds of more than 250 miles per hour and sells new for about $2 million. One night, Teodorin parked his toy near the entrance of L'Ermitage, a favorite hangout where he'd gone for drinks. When he saw gawkers stop to admire it, he sent Giacalone back to Malibu by cab so Giacalone could drive back his second Bugatti to park next to it.

Teodorin's household staff included drivers, housekeepers, caretakers, estate managers, executive assistants, chefs, landscaping crews, and two security teams staffed with off-duty and retired cops and guards from Equatorial Guinea. One security unit was based at the estate while a second, called the "chase team," tailed Teodorin on his late-night excursions into Malibu and beyond. The chauffeur Dragan Deletic recounted in his legal complaint that the chase team found it nearly impossible to tail Teodorin when he took the wheel of one of his cars, because he'd speed through red lights and generally drive like a maniac. "One night I was required to follow him in the chase vehicle from the House of Blues, where he became extremely intoxicated," reads the complaint. "When I suggested he be driven home he refused and I was required to follow him [as he] swerved home up the Pacific Coast Highway." Deletic alleged that his duties included "cleaning bottles of urine left in the back of the car by Obiang."

Legal filings depict the "prince" as a nocturnal creature who generally slumbered until afternoon and sometimes as late as 9:00 P.M. Despite his Dracula-like aversion to daylight, employees were required to arrive at the estate by 9:00 A.M. Housekeeper Lily Panayotti's complaint said that while her boss slept she'd perform duties such as "cleaning and polishing the Property's enormous collection of silver and crystal." But she was not allowed to depart until Teodorin awoke and she'd cleaned his room, closet, and bathroom, which routinely required her to work until midnight. Panayotti said that she was allowed to use only one of the estate's sixteen bathrooms, and that she was fed only beans, corn, and a mixture of potatoes with sausage.

Upon rising and freshening up, he might watch movies or play video games, browse through magazines, or spend time on Facebook. Teodorin enjoyed outings to the Magic Mountain amusement park, especially riding the roller coaster, but rarely stirred in time to go. He dated a series of women, among them the rapper Eve, whom he designated as president, treasurer, and chief financial officer of Sweet Pink, one of his shell companies. In 2005, Teodorin threw a party for Eve aboard the *Tatoosh*, a 303-foot yacht that he rented from its owner, Microsoft cofounder Paul Allen. An account in the New York *Daily News* said Eve ultimately cooled on Teodorin after hearing of rumors that his father was an accused cannibal who had eaten his political rivals.

Other companions included Tamala Jones, who appeared in such movies as *Booty Call* and *Confessions of a Call Girl* and later "starred in the ABC series *Castle*, and Lindsey Evans, who was named Miss Louisiana Teen USA in 2008, when she was eighteen (though she was soon stripped of her crown after she ran out on a $46.07 bill at a restaurant in her hometown of Blanchard) and Playmate of the Month in

October 2009. Teodorin would drop off and pick up Evans at the Playboy Mansion, where he was a regular and she had a job as eye candy at parties.

Teodorin's friends included Janet Jackson, a frequent visitor to the estate and occasional traveling companion. Her brother Jermaine was also an acquaintance. One well-placed source told me he turned up at the estate the day after the death of his brother Michael to borrow a Rolls-Royce Phantom to drive to the funeral.[10]

The guest list at Teodorin's mansion invariably included an assortment of high-heeled, miniskirt-clad women procured from escort agencies, according to my interviews with former employees. Veronique Guillem's complaint alleged that she had to "babysit" Teodorin's hired companions to minimize "damage [to] the property," which required her to "remain until early in the morning when they would leave." Former driver Giacalone said in this legal filing that he was required to be "on call 24/7 to fulfill any bizarre whim [of] the billionaire playboy" and that his job included managing Obiang's "various romantic interests, including booking their flights, managing conflicts, [and] taking them on elaborate shopping sprees."

Rae Cortina, a former executive assistant, said in her legal complaint that Teodorin once left behind at the mansion an escort who demanded cab fare to go home. Cortina called him and he gave the okay but subsequently refused to reimburse her, saying that she had not "submitted a check request" prior to giving the women money to pay the cab. Cortina's October 2010 complaint also charged that Teodorin had once called her to the foot of a staircase and stood above her wearing nothing but an open robe, one leg draped atop the banister. This was one of two times that Teodorin displayed "full frontal nudity" in her presence, the former assistant charges, prompting her to seek damages for "Intentional Infliction of Emotional Stress" on top of unpaid wages.

Charles Hagins, another former employee, was hired as estate manager but treated like a butler and go-fer, he told me during a conversation at the black-and-white marbled bar of the Beverly Wilshire Hotel. Hagins, who was then sixty (and died soon afterwards), had deep, watery blue eyes. Teodorin, he said, would call him at home in the middle of the night and demand that he bring him a bottle of wine or a hamburger from In-N-Out. "When someone comes through these gates, they're in Equatorial Guinea," Teodorin told him when he complained about the way he treated employees.

Giacalone's unofficial duties included accompanying his boss's girlfriends on elaborate shopping sprees. He also said the Dolce & Gabbana store on Rodeo Drive periodically dispatched a sales associate and tailor to Teodorin's estate in a van packed with racks of merchandise for his viewing, and would close off its second-floor showroom when his girlfriends came in to shop. Giacalone said he escorted one who racked up about eighty thousand dollars in purchases, including bronze and red dresses that cost nearly seven thousand dollars apiece. Giacalone paid the tab from a Nike shoebox filled with shrink-wrapped bills.

For nights on the town, Teodorin and his crew rarely strayed beyond Beverly Hills or Hollywood. His favorite spots were Crustacean, where he'd order piles of crab and garlic noodles; Katana, where he'd spend thousands of dollars for sushi; and Hop Li, a restaurant on Santa Monica Boulevard whose shark fin soup he swore by as the best cure after binging. At L'Ermitage, the boutique hotel in Beverly Hills, he'd rent a suite for a few hours of partying or get a table at the ground-floor patio.

As with Pippi Longstocking and her bottomless chest of gold coins, Teodorin never ran short of cash. Thanks to his diplomatic passport, Teodorin routinely carried as much as $1 million in cash into the country, the ICE documents allege. Several ex-employees said he had a bag the size of a small suitcase that was forever stuffed with stacks of fresh one-hundred-dollar bills.

Teodorin traveled on a Gulfstream V, which he bought in 2006 through a British Virgin Islands–registered shell called Ebony Shine International, Ltd. "He used it like a taxi," Giacalone said. "He'd fly alone or use it to pick up one passenger. Once he sent it from Rio to Los Angeles to bring back his barber." And Teodorin didn't travel light. He bought a fifteen-seat cargo van and had the seats taken out to fit his collection of Louis Vuitton luggage.

Records compiled by FlightAware, a firm that tracks private and commercial air traffic, show that Teodorin's ministerial duties took him to such vital destinations as Las Vegas, where a July 2009 bill for the presidential suite at the Four Seasons—made out to "Prince Teodoro Nguema Obiang"—showed a rate of five thousand dollars per night; to Miami, where he docked one of his two Nor-Tech 5000 speedboats. During a trip to the latter on New Year's

Eve 2006, Teodorin and a young female escort stayed at the Delano Hotel on South Beach, where the bill came to $250,000, according to a confidential source with direct knowledge of the vacation. That included the rental of three beachfront cabanas and expenses run up by the eight guests he flew in from Los Angeles, including his hairdresser. For three days, Teodorin and his companions ordered a steady supply of Johnny Walker Blue and completely depleted the hotel's supply of Dom Perignon Rose.

Teodorin's international destinations included Monaco, Bermuda, Nice, the Dominican Republic, and Brazil, where he has attended numerous Carnival celebrations. In 2010, according to a story in the Brazilian press, he rented the best suite at a luxury hotel in Copacabana. "He spent heavily on Brazilian women," the story said. "He burned through more than $100,000 reais [the equivalent of about $60,000 at the time] on presents." The previous year, Teodorin leased a yacht for Carnival and invited dozens of people to join him in Rio.

His fall 2009 month-long jaunt to Maui stands out for debauched luxury. Teodorin flew on the Gulfstream V and chartered a separate plane for household employees that included Giacalone, a security team, and a chef. (He brought in his French chef from Paris as well.) He shipped four cars to Maui—a Bugatti, a Lamborghini, a Rolls-Royce Phantom Coupé, and a Ferrari—three motorcycles, and one of the Nor-Techs.

Teodorin lodged at the Grand Wailea Resort, paying seven thousand dollars a night for a suite there, and rented a beachfront estate through a firm called Tropical Villa

Vacations, where he put up a revolving cast of escorts. "Most of them stayed for a few days and were replaced," recalled Giacalone, who picked the women up from the airport and generally coordinated their comings and goings. "He'd tell me to get rid of that one and bring this one. Take this one to Louis Vuitton, but don't let her spend more than five thousand dollars."

Teodorin would often schedule an early morning meeting with Giacalone and lay out grand plans for the day—a helicopter ride or a beach outing or touring—but then he'd go back to bed and sleep most of the day. There was one memorable outing, however. The gaudy orange, purple, and yellow Nor-Tech was shipped via Honolulu, where it fell off of a trailer and required repairs. It finally arrived in Maui during the last week of the trip, but the leaded fuel it required wasn't sold on the island, so Giacalone arranged to fly in fuel at a cost of six hundred dollars per barrel, which took two more days to arrive.

A local man was hired to pilot the Nor-Tech, his major qualification being that he was willing to work for only $150 for the day. Teodorin took a few girls with him on the ride, but there was only enough fuel for a fifteen-minute outing. Shortly after the "captain" dropped off the passengers and went to moor the boat, Giacalone received a frantic phone call. "He [the captain] was desperate," Giacalone said. "The boat was sinking." It turned out that the repair work in Honolulu had been done improperly and there was a small hole in the side of the boat that caused it to capsize.

The incident attracted quite a bit of attention and was

commented on by several posters at an online boating forum, thehulltruth.com. One wrote:

> I still have not be able to confirm where the guy is from, but money is not a problem. Yesterday, when it was time to drive the boat, the prince showed up at the ramp in his Bugatti ... Between the car, the boat, the royal aides (including four absolutely stunning foxes) with him, they were quite an image at the tiny ramp.

A special team had to be flown in from Honolulu to salvage the boat, an operation that required a helicopter and several trucks.

Total charges at the Grand Wailea topped three hundred thousand dollars. The bill for the rental property to house the girls came in at more than sixty thousand dollars.

Of all of Teodorin's mad extravagances, though, nothing compares to his plans to build the world's second-largest superyacht. Tim Heywood, one of the world's most renowned yacht designers, completed the drawings for Project Zen, as it was dubbed, in late 2008. Teodorin selected Kusch Yachts to oversee construction (motto: "We don't just build yachts that you use, we create a dream that you live"), which builds at a shipyard on the Elbe River in northern Germany.

The vessel's basic design was completed in December 2009, and the original delivery date was set for three years later. Kusch employees who spoke to a Global Witness investigator said that Teodorin's yacht was slated for 387 feet and would house a cinema, a restaurant, a bar, a swimming pool, and a $1.3 million security system complete with floor-motion sensors, photoelectric barriers, and fingerprint door openers. Its total contract price was approximately $380 million, which would have made it the world's second most expensive yacht, behind Russian oligarch Roman Abramovich's $1.2 billion Eclipse.

Teodorin's superyacht was never delivered, possibly because news leaked about his plans in 2011. At the time, the Information and Press Bureau for Equatorial Guinea's government said that if the order had gone ahead Teodorin "would have bought it with income from his private business activities and he would not in any case have bought it with funds derived from sources of illegal financing or corruption."

America has been one long party for Teodorin, but the Justice Department lawsuit seeking to seize his American assets suggest his day of wine and roses might finally be coming to an end. The lawsuit (whose outcome is still undecided as of this writing) is an important test case, because the US has shown it can take action when it wants to shut down terrorist financing or starve regimes, such as Iran, of investment and trade, but it has done little to stop sitting dictators—especially oil-rich dictators—and their families from using America to stash their assets. Washington generally avoids the potential foreign policy fallout that comes from pressuring friendly states to clean up their acts on human rights and corruption. Yet when the Obiang lawsuit was filed, a top Justice Department official declared that "the United States will not be a hiding place for the ill-gotten riches of the world's corrupt leaders."

The Justice Department's complaint is also a crucial test, because if the United States government can't win a case involving the Obiang clan, it might as well stop trying to hold corrupt dictators accountable. The message to tyrants and oligarchs will be "Come here and spend without fear that we'll confiscate any of your ill-gotten gains."

Yet even if the Justice Department wins its case, the same legal loopholes Teodorin used to accumulate his fortune here remain open. And hence despots and crooks will continue to bring their money to America, not only for prestige, but also because our corporate secrecy laws, like those of Switzerland and Luxembourg, make it almost impossible for law enforcement agencies to figure out who has money sheltered here.

The primary legal shortcoming is that many jurisdictions—from the Cayman Islands to the great majority of American states—don't require companies to disclose their true beneficial owners (as opposed to their registered owners, who serve as fronts). Dictators and despots can therefore easily hide their assets: Instead of buying property in their names, the mansion they want will instead be bought and owned by, for example, a Panamanian trust controlled by a Bahamian corporation that's run by a company registered in Liechtenstein.

For years Senator Levin of Michigan has advocated reforms that would require companies registered in the United States to reveal their beneficial owners. The World Bank, which found that America is the top destination for corrupt politicians trying to set up shell companies to access the financial system, supports the same goals.

Yet Levin's bill has gone nowhere, thanks to opposition from the United States Chamber of Commerce, the American Bar Association, and the state of Delaware, America's premier tax haven, where corporations outnumber people. "You can no longer open an account at a respectable bank merely with a suitcase of cash," the *Economist* has written in an editorial. "Let the same apply to starting a limited company." As long as those loopholes remain open there is nothing to prevent future Teodorins from laundering their money in the United States and using the country as their personal shopping mall just as he has.

Even more troubling is that the Washington–Malabo oil alliance is likely to survive the Justice Department lawsuit no matter the outcome. US oil companies remain the bulwark of Equatorial Guinea's economy, and President Obiang, while having expressed his annoyance with the Justice Department, shows no lessening of affection for them.

That means the US government may soon find that it needs to deal far more directly with Teodorin in the future. In a clear sign of his political ascendancy, his doting father named him vice president of the ruling party in 2011. Given the size of his country's oil reserves, he's going to have leverage—and cash—for a long time to come.

To ensure that Equatorial Guinea stays within the reasonable limits of Washington's good graces, Obiang has hired reams of American lobbyists and PR specialists, retaining at various times a dozen different firms, including some of the Beltway's most prominent hired guns and media polishers. Millions more have been spent by international oil companies lobbying for the Obiang regime. ExxonMobil spent more than $6 million on that task in 2008 alone.

Lobbyists who have been on the Obiang dole include a former special counsel to Bill Clinton, Lanny Davis (who also represented the 2009 Honduran coup plotters and the human-rights-abusing leader of Ivory Coast Laurent Gbagbo, who triggered a civil war by refusing to step down after losing the 2010 election there). In exchange for $1 million per year, Davis promised to "improve perceptions" of Equatorial Guinea with the American media and government. In his pitch to the dictator, he blamed the country's negative image on "actions of the old regime," this presumably a reference to the Macías government, which Obiang had toppled more than three decades earlier. Davis's contract said he could offer "international monitoring and validation" for the presidential election of 2009, though that would be at an additional cost. It's not clear if Davis followed through on his offer of electoral "validation," but he told the *New York Times* of Obiang, "I've kidded him he'd do better to win by 51 percent than 98 percent."[11]

The government's most recent lobbyists include Qorvis Communications, which for fifteen thousand dollars per month provided "message development and refinement" and a "proactive media relations engagement strategy." Among other things, that paid for a steady stream of news releases highlighting all manner of heartwarming news about Equatorial Guinea, from the Obiang government's alleged support for animal conservation to native daughter Matinga Ragatz being named Michigan's teacher of the year. Teodorin separately paid the firm $55,000 per month to help polish his image, lobbying disclosure reports say.

One summer evening I met two of Teodorin's PR handlers from Qorvis, Matt J. Lauer and Seth Pietras, at a bar in Washington. The two men unknotted their ties in unison after slipping onto a couch and ordering drinks. Allegations of human rights abuses in Equatorial Guinea are highly exaggerated, they said, citing as evidence their experience during a trip to the country. "We could walk around at night and talk with people and no one interfered with us," said Lauer. "No one is saying there are no problems, but it's not North Korea." They were similarly miffed about Teodorin's reputation as a high-rolling kleptocrat, saying that officials from a number of energy-rich countries also live lavishly while their client was unfairly singled out. Pietras noted that George W. Bush had reportedly been a drinker and partier as a younger man before becoming more serious. Teodorin, he offered, "is at the point where he's thinking about his legacy."

If so, some serious soul-searching is in order—and not just by Teodorin.

3

The Traders: Glencore

You can be the smartest trader in the world and you still can't make money without access to oil. Fortunately, there is always access if you are willing to pay enough cash.

—Swiss commodity broker

When Glencore, the world's biggest commodities brokerage firm, went public in May 2011, the initial public offering (IPO) on the London and Hong Kong stock exchanges made headlines for weeks in the trade-industry press, which devoted endless columns to the company's astonishing valuation of nearly $60 billion—higher than Boeing or Ford Motor Company. The massive new wealth turned the nearly five hundred employees into overnight multimillionaires and made billionaires of at least five senior executives, including CEO Ivan Glasenberg. "We are not going to change the way we operate," vowed Glasenberg, who had started as a lowly coal trader for the Swiss firm nearly three decades earlier and, with the IPO, immediately became one of Europe's richest men. "Being public will have absolutely no effect on the business."

Going public forced the firm to pull back the curtain on its famously secretive doings, and what it revealed shocked even seasoned commodities traders. Glencore turned out to be far more globally dominant than analysts had realized. According to its 1,637-page IPO prospectus: the company controlled more than half the international tradable market in zinc and copper and about a third of the world's seaborne coal; was one of the world's largest grain export-ers, with about 9 percent of the global market; and handled 3 percent of daily global oil consumption for customers ranging from state-owned energy companies in Brazil and India to American multinationals such as ExxonMobil and Chevron. All of which, the prospectus said, helped the firm post revenues of $186 billion in 2011 and employ some fifty-five thousand people in at least forty countries, gen-erating an average return on equity of 38 percent, about three times higher than that of the gold-standard invest-ment bank Goldman Sachs in 2010.

Since the IPO, the company has only gotten vaster in scale by making a series of acquisitions, among them a merger with Canada's biggest grain trader, Viterra, and a $90 billion takeover of Xstrata, a global mining giant in which it already held a 34 percent stake. Thanks to the latter deal Glencore will rule over an "empire stretching from the Sahara to South Africa," as *Africa Confidential* put it. As it is, Glencore already trades, manufactures, refines, ships, or stores at least ninety commodities in some three dozen countries.

Glencore's physical presence in the United States is

modest; it has minor holdings in a few American companies and an office in Stamford, Connecticut, that helps run its oil and gas trading business. But its global market power and reach make its operations important to American policy makers as well as to the public. "Wherever you turn in the world of commodities, you bump into Glencore," says Nicholas Shaxson, author of *Treasure Islands*, a book about tax havens and an associate fellow at the British think tank Chatham House. "It is twice as big as Koch Industries, and it has an unhealthy grip on some of the world's most important commodity markets, with influence that stretches from Texas to Tehran to Taipei."

Peter Brandt, a longtime commodities trader, echoes that assessment. "Glencore is at the center of the raw material world," he told me. "Within this world there are giants, and Glencore is becoming a giant among giants." China's manufacturing base, one of the world's economic engines, "could not exist without Glencore, because it is dependent on raw material imports, many of which Glencore plays a major role in trading and producing," he added.

If the IPO shed light on Glencore's assets and influence, it did not make clear just how Glencore, founded four decades ago by Marc Rich, a defiant friend of dictators and spies who later became one of the world's richest fugitives, achieved this kind of global dominance. The answer is at once simpler and far more complicated than it appears. Like all traders, it makes its money at the margins, but Glencore, even more so than its competitors, profits by working in the globe's most marginal business regions and often at the margins of what is legal.

This means: operating in countries where many multinationals fear to tread; building walls made of shell corporations, complex partnerships, and offshore accounts to obscure transactions; and working with shady intermediaries who help the company gain access to resources and curry favor with the corrupt, resource-rich regimes that have made Glencore so fabulously wealthy. "We conduct whatever due diligence is appropriate in each situation to ensure we operate in line with Glencore Corporate Practice," was spokesman Simon Buerk's terse reply when I asked how the firm chooses business partners and local representatives.

Given the nature of its business, there's simply no other way for a company like Glencore to thrive. "Unlike the case with many industries, minerals and energy are often owned by the state in Third World countries," says Michael Ross, author of *The Oil Curse* and a professor at the University of California, Los Angeles. "And in a number of countries where Glencore operates, doing business means putting money into the pockets of repressive governments and corrupt rulers. In some of those places ... it's hard to draw a line between what's legally corrupt and what's not." Traders like Glencore—which Reuters once called "the biggest company you never heard of"—are largely invisible to the public. One obvious reason is that, with the exception of post-IPO Glencore, all the big traders are privately held and not subject to corporate disclosure laws. Another is that energy companies that produce oil, like ExxonMobil and Shell, also sell it at the corner gas station. Consumers don't have that sort of interaction with trading companies, so they get less scrutiny.

Furthermore, oil traders are not obliged to disclose the amounts they trade, and the firms operate under different names and affiliates. Jack Blum, an attorney and former Senate counsel who played a key role in investigations into Bank of Credit and Commerce International (BCCI), said regulating hedge funds would be easier than keeping tabs on traders. "They operate through a maze of subsidiaries, and it's virtually impossible to know who they are trading with and how much and at what prices," he told me.

Glencore's effective global tax rate for 2010 was just 9.3 percent, in large part because nearly half its forty-six subsidiaries are incorporated in "secrecy jurisdictions," opaque financial havens like the Netherlands, according to a report by the nongovernmental organization (NGO) Publish What You Pay. Glencore's Rotterdam-registered Finges Investment is worth $18 billion, but doesn't have a single employee, according to corporate records filed in the Netherlands. Finges, a Dutch financial expert told me, is "nothing more than a piece of financial engineering."

When it comes to the media, oil traders consciously seek to stay out of the public spotlight. Sylvain Besson of *Le Temps*, a major daily newspaper in Geneva, describes a "culture of discretion" that prevails across the industry. "It's a hard world to penetrate," he said. "Banks will take very public stands, but not traders. It is the most discreet profession, and we have many discreet professions. They prefer we not write about them."

Glencore in particular is known for its incredibly secretive corporate culture. One source compared the company to the CIA. Another said, "It's like a church. They buy loyalties; no one ever talks."

Traders have enormous political power, and because they are less regulated and scrutinized are able to do things that most energy-producing companies wouldn't dare. In 2007, Glencore effectively helped bankroll Ivory Coast strongman Laurent Gbagbo by discreetly providing his cash-strapped state oil company with an $80 million loan that was to be repaid with future exports. Gbagbo was overthrown four years later, at which point the loan had been renewed three times, and the state company, Petroci, still owed Glencore around 650,000 barrels that were worth about $70 million.

During the early stages of the 2011 revolt that drove Libya's Muammar Gaddafi from power, Vitol, one of Glencore's chief competitors, secretly delivered (on credit) hundreds of millions of dollars worth of fuel to the opposition. The grateful rebels awarded Vitol the first contract to lift Libyan crude after the country resumed exporting oil following Gaddafi's overthrow.

Going public is unlikely to change the broad business model created and perfected by Rich, who, before his controversial pardon by US president Bill Clinton, was a legendary fugitive, a regular fixture (along with Osama bin Laden) on the FBI's Most Wanted list. The new Glencore will be like the Glencore of old—only much, much bigger. In today's superheated market for natural resources, driven by markets such as Brazil, China, and India, Glencore wants to grow—and in a major way. Already the world's biggest middleman, it now wants to control the entire business chain, from mines and smelters to storage facilities for finished products, and from pumping oil to shipping it to refineries, while trading and hedging all along the way.

Take copper, for example: Glencore mines it, refines it, transports it, and makes wire and other finished products. "That's one way that Glencore makes so much money," a Geneva-based industry source told me. "When you are vertically integrated you make more at every step. The money stays in the same pocket."

Another way Glencore makes so much money is by leveraging information to take advantage of the wild swings that have marked global commodity prices in recent years, with oil yo-yoing from $147 a barrel in mid-2008 down to $40 later that year.[1] Poor countries that sell commodities often end up losers when prices go down—like Zambia, which in recent years has been intermittently walloped by a combination of rising prices for agricultural products and sharply falling prices for copper and the other mineral exports on which it depends. But Glencore, like a casino where the house always wins, "benefits directly from the volatility," as Deutsche Bank noted cheerfully in a report issued prior to the IPO for potential investors.

Michael Masters, founder of both a global investment management firm and of Better Markets, a Washington DC–based group established to promote transparency in the financial markets, takes a far less rosy view. He described Glencore as an "active predatory force" that has an inordinate influence on the price of raw materials that are important to the US and global economy. "They are smart and good and know how to use information to exploit other investors," he told me. "When they're selling you don't want to be buying, and when they're buying you don't want to be selling."

Still, the real secret to Glencore's success is operating in markets that scare off more risk-averse companies that fear running afoul of corporate governance laws in the United States and the European Union. In fact, those markets are precisely where the future of the company lies. Deutsche Bank identified Glencore's "key drivers" as: the growth of copper in the Democratic Republic of the Congo; coal in Colombia; oil and natural gas in Equatorial Guinea; and gold in Kazakhstan. All are places with a heady, dangerous mix of extraordinary natural wealth and various degrees of instability, violence, and strongman leaders. Glencore's experience and adeptness operating in these "frontier regions" and "challenging political jurisdictions"—Deutsche Bank's delicate euphemisms for countries known for corruption, autocracy, and human rights abuses—is central, the investment firm wrote, to Glencore's "significant growth potential."

The oil trading business—by which firms negotiate and purchase output from energy-producing nations, find buyers, arrange financing, and charter tankers to ship oil—didn't exist in its current form until after the 1973 Israeli-Arab war. Until then a few Western multinational companies dominated the oil business: They controlled the fields, the ships, and the refineries. Meanwhile, the United States and a handful of other industrial powers consumed 90 percent of exports, and so there existed a rough pipeline that moved global oil from the Third World to the First World. Daniel Yergin writes in his book *The Quest*:

> Most of the global oil trade took place inside each of the integrated oil companies, among their various operating units ... Throughout this long journey, the oil remained largely within the borders of the company. This was what was meant by "integration." It was considered the natural order of the business, the way the oil industry was to be managed.

The system broke up because producer companies got tired of bring ripped off by the multinationals and their home governments. One way they fought back was through the Organization of the Petroleum Exporting Countries (OPEC), which was founded in 1965 but only closely coordinated members' output to determine production after the Yom Kippur War. The conflict prompted OPEC to launch its embargo against the West, leading to an explosion in the price of oil. While the West viewed this as unfair collusion and political manipulation of oil prices, OPEC producers understandably saw it as a means of gaining a fairer share of the profits from the global energy business.

The emergence of independent trading also allowed producer countries to alter the balance of power. "The major companies were screwing the producer countries," a Geneva oil trader said. "They said, we're taking your oil, and we'll tell you what it's worth, and we'll refine it and sell it. But that all changed the day a trader turned up and said, I'll pay you twenty-one dollars instead of the twenty dollars they're paying you."

Oil trading proved to be hugely profitable, and before long the major companies had created their own trading wings. With the run up in global demand of the past few decades, the market has gotten far bigger and more lucrative. Glencore was valued at less than $1 billion in the mid-1990s, about one sixtieth of its value at the time of the IPO.[2]

Traders have flocked to Switzerland ever since the early days of the industry. The reasons for that choice are numerous, among them the country's long record as a financial haven that offers strict rules on bank and corporate secrecy and its weak business regulation. For years Swiss authorities did not prosecute bribery, and banks were not subject to money-laundering laws. Some rules have been tightened, but commodity traders and financial intermediaries are still largely unregulated. "It's a light touch here," one Swiss trader told me during a trip I made to the country in 2011.[3] "There are rules, but they are not always applied."

For traders, another major advantage of operating in Switzerland has been the country's political neutrality and its reluctance to enforce international sanctions and embargoes. Swiss-based traders supplied oil to the South African apartheid state despite a UN embargo against Pretoria. Switzerland joined the UN in 2002, but is not a member of the European Union, and applies EU sanctions selectively. Ten years later Vitol bought fuel oil from Iran and offered it to Chinese buyers—and allegedly blended it with fuel oil from Europe to hide its origin—despite an EU embargo on oil trading with Iran. But Swiss-based firms could evade the embargo, because the government, citing unspecified "foreign policy reasons," rejected the ban.

Low corporate and personal taxes are another draw. Switzerland even offers special tax arrangements to attract rich individuals (and indirectly their companies) through a simple process known as the *Forfait fiscal*. The list of *Forfait* recipients and details of the individual deals are kept secret, but the total number of beneficiaries is public. Until a decade ago, about two thousand people had negotiated individual tax deals with Swiss authorities; by 2012 that number has climbed to about six thousand.

The names of a few recipients have leaked and include a number of big oil traders, such as Gennady Timchenko of Gunvor, a Russian firm with close ties to the Kremlin. Another person granted a *Forfait* was Chechen oligarch Bulat Chagaev, an intimate associate of ex-warlord and President Ramzan Kadyrov, who owns two Geneva-based firms, Dagmara Trading and Envergure Holding, which reportedly oversee his oil and gas trading, real estate, and construction empires. During an interview with Swiss national television, Chagaev declined to state the size of his fortune—"I don't know as I never count my money, nor that of others"—or to comment on allegations that he had purchased a major Swiss soccer team as a vehicle to launder money. "I don't know what clean or dirty money is," he said of the latter charge. "Money has no family name or country; it's just money."

The political influence of the financial and trading sectors is also reassuring to commodity traders and other investors. "Creating favorable conditions to attract money from abroad is the basic strength of the whole Swiss system," says Besson of *Le Temps*. "Traders don't often take a highly visible political role—the banks are the most powerful visible lobby—but the political world is very sensitive to the broad needs of the offshore sector, including traders. Their influence is constant if not visible."

"It's a banana republic in extremis," says Oliver Classen, from the Berne Declaration, a NGO that tracks traders, of their political influence.

Geneva is now reckoned to have surpassed London as the world's biggest center for physical oil trading, and hundred of traders are based in or have major operations there. These include American corporate behemoths such as Cargill, state energy firms from Ukraine and Azerbaijan, and the trading houses of multinationals such as Total of France.

Independent traders are heavily represented in Switzerland as well. Vitol, which pled guilty for paying illegal commissions to Saddam Hussein's government under the United Nations oil-for-food program, also has a checkered past when it comes to hiring shady middlemen. In the mid-1990s the company paid Željko Ražnatović— better known as Arkan, the Serbian career criminal and paramilitary leader who the UN later indicted for crimes against humanity—$1 million to serve as a consultant on a deal in the former Yugoslavia.

During the huge energy price run-up in 2008, the Commodity Futures Trading Commission labeled Vitol a "speculator" that bought oil contracts to hold as investments instead of delivering fuel. At one point during the price spike Vitol held more than 10 percent of all oil contracts bought and sold on the New York Mercantile Exchange.

Frenchman Jean Claude Gandur founded Addax, another giant with offices in Geneva. Over the years it won various contracts in Africa and the Middle East by partnering with locals tied to ruling families and leaders. "In these parts of the world you are invariably going to be dealing with people connected to someone powerful in the ruling elite," Michael Ebsary, a firm executive, once explained. "That's just the way it is." Addax also has major interests in Iraqi Kurdistan, including oil fields and a refinery. In 2009, Sinopec of China bought Addax in a move seen as a sign of Beijing's ambitions to lock up its growing global energy needs.

Trafigura, one of many trading companies established by veterans of Marc Rich & Company, gained notoriety in 2006 for dumping toxic waste in the Ivory Coast (see p. 6). Through at least late 2011 Trafigura was selling fuel to Bashar al-Assad's regime in Syria as it intensified a bloody crackdown on its opposition and the country lurched toward chaos and civil war.[4]

Gunvor of Russia, which swiftly grew to become the world's third-largest oil trader, was founded by its owners—Torbjörn Törnqvist and Gennady Timchenko—as a series of mailbox companies in the British Virgin Isles, Cyprus, and the Netherlands. They moved the firm to Geneva in 2003, the same year that the Russian government took over Yukos and tossed CEO Mikhail Khodorkovsky into jail. Gunvor took off after that; its rivals say the company has thrived due to favorable treatment from Vladimir Putin. International press reports have periodically suggested that Timchenko is a front for Putin.

Uniquely among the giant trading firms, Glencore is located in Zug, a charming canton a few hours from Geneva and just north of the Alps. This is where Marc Rich founded the firm, and today Glencore operates there out of a gleaming white steel-and-glass headquarters.

Zug's population of residents and registered companies both hover around twenty-seven thousand, and the corporate tax rate averages around 15 percent, low even by Swiss standards and far below top rates in the US. Burger King Holdings, Adidas, Siemens, and Transocean Ltd.—owner of the Deepwater Horizon drilling rig that sank in the Gulf of Mexico in 2010—are among the multinational giants headquartered in Zug. Income taxes are also low, and in Rüschlikon, where Glasenberg lives not far from the Glencore headquarters, citizens voted to drop them further after the IPO, as his fortune at that point had swelled to an estimated $7.3 billion and was so huge that his taxes alone were sufficient to fund the town's entire budget.

The conventional view of oil traders is that they make money by leveraging information to buy cheap and sell high. They are, as Daniel Yergin writes in his book *The Quest*, "nimble players who ... with hair-trigger timing, dart in and out to take advantage of the smallest anomalies and mispricings."

During a trip to Switzerland in 2011 I interviewed half a dozen traders; all would speak only off the record, given the sensitivity of their business and their forthrightness about it. All of them spoke of the range of expertise required to succeed in the business, from hedging and currencies to shipping, logistics, and pricing. "There's a lot of know-how involved," one former trader, who worked for Glencore in Africa, told me. "Not everyone knows how to paddle up shit creek without oars. It won't work if you're sitting at a desk in London; you have to be down there."

Yet all of them acknowledged that political connections were even more vital than technical expertise. "The oil business has now and then involved sharing the benefits," this person put it euphemistically. "It always comes down to the same thing."

The right contacts are just as important on the downstream side as they are upstream. One trader told me about his company's local office in an Asian country, which sold refined products to major petrochemical plants. His office, he said wryly, was staffed by "a bunch of drunks." Their chief strategy for finding deals and beating out their competitors was to "wine and dine the procurement guys"—karaoke nights were a particular favorite—at the plants they sold to. "Through those relationships, we knew the procurement schedule at the big buyers," he said. "It wasn't a straight market play; it was a play based on friendships. It's not a black-and-white world."

Another trader, who bought and sold oil exclusively in Africa, met me at his elegant office on the outskirts of Geneva and offered a curious defense of bribery. He led me past an open area, where about six traders were scanning information onto their computers and into a large conference room that had a beautiful wood table, polished to a waxy sheen. Most Westerners misunderstood the concept of corruption, he told me after a secretary had served us espressos in small white cups. "In a lot of Third World countries there is no functioning government and no tax collection, so the head of state gives a mine or an oil concession to a chief or a minister and tells him to go feed his family. What NGOs call corruption is a system of distribution; it's an inefficient system, but it's a way of putting money into the country."

He acknowledged that companies sometimes arranged payoffs, legal or otherwise, to win favor with Third World leaders, but argued that this was fundamentally no different from what happens in Europe and the United States. "If you want to talk to a senator, you give money to his PAC. And look at Goldman Sachs, which hires every ex- and future secretary of the treasury. It's the same shit. You pay for access."

"But that's a form of corruption too, isn't it?" I asked. Wasn't he just arguing that the West had its own skewed "systems of distribution"? And what about what the other traders had told me? If you don't have access to oil, you can't make money, and so he, like all traders, tried hard to get better access than his competitors, even if it meant cutting a few corners. Wasn't oil trading fundamentally a dirty business?

He waved this off impatiently: "Yes, you need oil, but there is always someone who can sell you it. And yes, there have been traders who have broken embargoes and made a lot of money, even though, putting aside the moral arguments, they probably didn't do anything illegal if they were

Swiss traders. But everything has become more transparent because of the globalization of ethics. Today no one will sell to Iran, except China. The banks won't lend the money. Even fifteen years ago you could send a rust bucket to Africa. Today all tankers are high quality. There is a tendency toward specificity of standards in a global market."

His view was that oil trading is no different than trading in other goods and commodities. "It's really about transportation," he said, as his secretary poured another round of espresso. "Trading is just moving a product from an area of surplus to an area of deficit. You are selling a product that is the same everywhere else. The only reason people buy it from you is because it's cheaper. You have no reason to be loyal and buy from one company."

He also dismissed my suggestion that traders profited from speculation and price gouging. "Speculators don't make the market; they amplify trends, and if they go against the market they end up getting smacked," he said. By way of illustration he noted that commodities trading boomed in the 1970s, busted in the 1980s and 1990s, and boomed again in the 2000s. Gold prices tanked through the 1990s, and no amount of manipulation would have changed that; gold soared in the 2000s "because of the stupidity of the US in Iraq and other reasons, not because of speculators." With regard to oil, traders might affect daily fluctuations, but big price movements up or down were caused by broader trends.

Others I spoke with acknowledged—some with satisfaction and others dismay—that traders played a more substantial role in the speculation that has agitated oil markets in recent years. I took a fifty-minute train ride from Geneva to the town of Montreux, at the foot of the Alps, to meet with a retired commodities broker who got his start in the 1980s trading cement, rice, and spices before moving on to buying and selling oil and refined products. We had lunch across the street from the train station at the Grand Hotel.

Since the oil shocks of the 1970s, the prevailing analysis has tended to describe oil prices in strict supply-and-demand terms, often placed in a geopolitical context. If it wasn't conflict in the Middle East that was jacking up prices, it was devious oil cartels tinkering with the spigot, Hugo Chávez nationalizing refineries, rebels in the Niger Delta blowing up pipelines, or demand from the emerging middle class in India and China.

But for the past seven years the price of oil had been swinging wildly in the face of contradictory supply and demand data. After floating in the $10 to $40 per barrel range for almost twenty years, it started to climb sharply in 2005, when it crossed $70. After falling back a bit, it spiked to $140 in the middle of 2008. (On September 22 of that year, the price actually jumped $25 in a single day.) But then the price fell off a cliff, down to a Clinton-era price of $30, in just six months. Within two years it had tripled again.

A cause and effect of the big price swings is what my lunch companion called "the horrendous development" of a variety of hedging techniques and their growing sophistication.[5] At most trading companies, he explained, one desk handles the physical trade in oil and another handles the paper trade. The job of the latter is to hedge the sales of the former, but in the past few decades the ratio of the daily physical trade to the paper trade has gone from roughly 1 to 1 to 40 or even 50 to 1. "People are sitting there all day just buying and selling paper barrels," this person said. "Everyone knows we need better rules and regulations, but the people who are making money don't want the rules to change. Historically paper markets were created to facilitate trade by letting buyers and sellers hedge their bets. The intention was not for people to gamble or to give them the ability to manipulate the market, which is what happens today."

"That sounds conspiratorial," I said. "Is there a lot of collusion between the traders?"

"I'm not talking about a formal conspiracy, but these guys all know each other," he replied. "It's so easy to influence prices. If someone at one trader decides he's going to start selling one hundred million barrels of [oil], the market will obviously go down. No doubt if he makes a call to his friend, and that friend talks to his friend, in a few days everyone is selling, selling, selling—and the insiders sell early and make a giant profit."

My lunch companion had traded mostly in sub-Saharan Africa, but he had also closed deals in Algeria, Venezuela, Russia, and Libya. Not surprisingly, he had a fairly jaded view about the nature of the business. "Ten years ago, I'd get on a plane with money straight from the bank to spread around; that's how deals were done," he told me forthrightly. "Now you sign a contract with an offshore company that's owned by the relative of some government official you need. The company may not be strictly legitimate or conduct any real business for you, but everybody's happy. Western banks might want to know who the real owners of the offshore company are, and they will zero in on you if the firm is not legitimate. But in the Far East—Singapore, China, Hong Kong—banking is far less restrictive. The same is true on weapons deals and other big contracts. It's the way of the world."

But the most unapologetic cynicism came from two men with decades of experience in the oil trading business that I met for dinner one evening in Geneva. The first (a Frenchman whom I'll call Philippe) began his work career with French intelligence before moving to oil giant Elf. Now privatized and part of Total, Elf built a stronghold in Africa on the basis of massive bribes to political leaders. In 2003, three senior company executives were sentenced to jail for siphoning off corporate funds and making payoffs in what the *Guardian* described at the time as "the biggest political and corporate sleaze scandal to hit a Western democracy since the Second World War." "During the Elf years we had a lot of connections in Africa," Philippe told me at his beautiful home on the city's outskirts. "They are small countries, and you can get to know everyone; it's not hard to meet presidents." After leaving Elf, Phillippe in fact served as an adviser to several African presidents and to a variety of oil trading firms that do extensive business in Africa.

He and I drove to a restaurant called Au P'tit Bonheur. The temperature was mild and the sky clear, and we sat on a terrace that afforded a splendid view of the city's famous lake and the surrounding Alps. We were soon joined by his friend Alain (not his real name), an executive in the oil and gas industry who frequently deals with the trading houses. Whereas Philippe was dressed simply but elegantly in jeans, a brown-and-white checked shirt, and monogrammed tennis shoes, Alain favored more traditional business attire. "The oil business is a service-intense industry, which requires a lot of related expertise," he told me. "Networking is extremely important, and so is information. Geneva is a village; everyone I need to know is here."

Soon bottles of white wine and plates of food were brought to the table, beginning with foie gras and other appetizers and moving on to a main course of trout and grilled vegetables. "The problem for traders is, they need something to sell," Philippe said between forkfuls of food. "The major oil companies produce oil directly, so their trading wings have no problem. Russian traders have strong links home, so they also have no problem getting access to production. But independent traders don't produce their own oil, so if they want access they need to have special relations with the chiefs of state."

"Trading oil is built on money," Alain joined in. "If you get my volume, then you support me and I support you. Maybe that's a bit rough, but that's the way it is."

Alain offered what he called "the proof of the importance of politics and money." A business associate, he said, was familiar with the 2006 incident in which a Trafigura-leased ship carrying toxic waste was turned away in several European ports but was finally allowed to dump its contents at Abidjan in the Ivory Coast.

"Trafigura made a trading decision to get rid of that stuff, and in Holland there was no way to get rid of it, so they sent it to Africa," he said. "There was a scandal, but that didn't break the company's relationship with Ivory Coast. After everything died down, Trafigura started doing business with the government again, and does business with it now. Why? Money is changing hands. You'll never clean corruption from the system."

"The Chinese are strong in Africa because they make unconventional deals," Philippe added, as he called a waiter over to order dessert. "In countries like Equatorial Guinea, if you want a deal, it's simple: They get 50 percent. You have no choice."

After espresso and dessert were served—chocolate mousse topped with ice cream and berries—the table talk turned to the business and personal pleasures of living in Switzerland. "If it were only a question of taxes, you could do better offshore, but that doesn't give you the stability and security of Switzerland," Phillipe said, with a contented smile. "The services are excellent, and there are excellent international schools if you have kids. There's skiing, biking, and sailing. Life here is not so bad."

"We're all bandits here," Alain added. "You can be accepted as long as you bring a lot of money."

To which Philippe heartily agreed, saying: "You have to pay your parking and your taxes and respect your neighbors, but if you want to cut a deal with a bandit, it's OK."

*   *   *

Leveraging ties to dictators has always been at the heart of the business empire built by Rich, the Belgian-born US citizen who founded what would become Glencore in Switzerland in 1974. Undeniably brilliant, Rich started in 1954 as a mail clerk at Philipp Brothers, then the world's dominant commodities firm, and within two years had worked his way into the position of junior trader. His own politics were conservative, but money trumped ideology for Rich; he was just as willing to cut deals in fascist Spain—where he worked for a time at the company's Madrid office, which specialized in handling business in rough countries in Africa and the Middle East—as in communist Cuba, where Philipp Brothers had dispatched him soon after Fidel Castro took power. He went on to travel frequently to Havana, where, in addition to picking up a lifelong fondness for Cohiba Cigars, he did business in pyrite, copper, and nickel.

He and Pincus "Pinky" Green left Philipp Brothers in 1974 and established Marc Rich & Co. in the canton of Zug, Switzerland's most business-friendly tax and secrecy haven. From early on, Rich cultivated ties to monarchs and presidents, diplomats and intelligence agencies, especially Iran's SAVAK under the shah. During the Arab oil embargo of the early 1970s Rich brokered a deal by which Iran secretly supplied Israel, which proved to be a vital economic lifeline.[6] Rich also periodically lent a hand to the Mossad's clandestine operations, among them the evacuation of Ethiopian Jews to Israel in the 1980s.

Rich made a fortune by buying oil from Iran during the hostage crisis and from Libya when Ronald Reagan's administration imposed a trade embargo on Muammar Gaddafi's regime, as well as from supplying oil to apartheid South Africa. An inveterate sanctions-buster, Rich used offshore front companies and corporate cutouts to try to stay below the radar. He also pioneered the practice of commodity swaps, like the uranium-for-oil deals he brokered in the 1980s between apartheid South Africa and Iran. Such deals frequently caused him trouble with US authorities, and in 1983 Rich fled his home in New York to Switzerland just before the Justice Department issued an indictment against him and Green on charges of racketeering, illegal trading with Iran, and tax evasion. A House committee later described his business as "based largely on systematic bribes and kickbacks to corrupt local officials."

Still Rich continued to thrive, until he unsuccessfully tried to corner the global zinc market in 1992 and nearly bankrupted the firm with $172 million in losses, at which point he was forced out in a management buyout. The new directors renamed the company Glencore, reportedly short for Global Energy Commodities and Resources.

Rich's forced exit from Glencore and the US indictment hanging over his head had little impact on his business success. He created a new, independent firm and within a decade was trading 1.5 million barrels of oil a day, with an annual turnover of $30 billion. Then, in 2001, on Clinton's last day in office, the president granted Rich a controversial pardon[7] stemming from the eighteen-year-old indictment; critics argued that the pardon was connected to the generous contributions that Rich's ex-wife, Denise, made to a variety of Democratic causes, including Hillary Clinton's successful 2000 Senate campaign and the Clinton presidential library fund. A number of prominent American Jews and Israelis, including then prime minister Ehud Barak and former Mossad director general Shabtai Shavit, also pressed the White House on Rich's behalf.

After his forced departure from Glencore Rich retired to a lavish estate, La Villa Rose, on the shores of Lake Lucerne, but his influence continued to be felt at the firm and throughout the industry (Rich died in 2013). Glasenberg, the company's CEO since 2002, got his start under Rich as a coal trader and, like the man who mentored him, was a quick study. By the late 1980s, just a few years after he was hired, he was managing the firm's China and Hong Kong offices and had become one of Rich's most trusted lieutenants. At least four other top Glencore executives at the time of the IPO had joined the firm in the Marc Rich era. They've preserved a workaholic ethic at the top of the company and—as a London law firm representing the company warned in a letter sent to major British news outlets soon after the IPO—consider themselves "extremely private individuals."

This new leadership at Glencore wasn't about to alter the formula of the firm's success. In one post-Rich example, the company profited handsomely by dealing with Saddam Hussein under the 1996–2003 UN oil-for-food program, which allowed the Iraqi dictator to trade limited quantities of oil in exchange for humanitarian supplies. The UN's Independent Inquiry Committee reported in 2005 that Hussein had awarded special "allocations" to companies and individuals who were friendly to the regime. A

Glencore agent, Pakistani businessman Murtaza Lakhani, was a conspicuous regime sycophant who hosted a peace concert at his local villa just weeks before the 2003 US invasion. The UN committee determined that Glencore had paid surcharges and raised questions about lavish commissions Lakhani received. The Iraq Survey Group, the US-led fact-finding mission sent after the invasion, concluded that Glencore was "one of the most active purchasers" of oil under the oil-for-food program and had paid $3,222,780 in "illegal surcharges." Yet Glencore was not charged in the scandal after claiming it was unaware surcharges were being paid and that Lakhani's high fees reflected the extra risk of doing business with Iraq, not slush money for bribes.

And that's the heart of the Marc Rich formula: Access is money, and contacts on the ground mean access. The new Glencore, like the old one, relies on a network of fixers, middlemen, and business partners who have special access to key decision makers in the countries where it operates. In South Africa the company is represented by Ivor Ichikowitz, an arms and oil broker who "has made a career from turning political connections into profit," according to the *Mail & Guardian*. His ties to the African National Congress allowed Glencore "to secure primacy in government oil business that no other trader was able to," the newspaper said.

Ichikowitz grew rich by selling surplus South African armored vehicles elsewhere in Africa and in the Middle East. When Thabo Mbeki held power Ichikowitz formed a vast joint venture—its interests ranged from sugar to infrastructure—with the president's brother. In December 2010 he provided a jet to ferry current president Jacob Zuma to Lebanon and Kazakhstan for ANC fundraising and business meetings.

Oil trading contracts have long been a trough of patronage in Nigeria and provide the government with its single largest revenue stream. Glencore achieved its greatest influence under military dictator Sani Abacha but smoothly transitioned to civilian rule in 1999 by hiring agents with connections to incoming president Olusegun Obasanjo, who had been imprisoned under Abacha. More recently, Glencore's share of the market has declined, as its rivals have gained greater political influence. Glencore is, however, still authorized to lift sixty thousand barrels per day and is believed to obtain significantly more than that by buying oil from politically well-connected firms that have allocations of their own.

In postcommunist Romania, Glencore discreetly collaborated with a variety of murky partners and agents, some widely deemed to be gangsters. During the mid-2000s it used an Israeli agent named Yoav Stern, who also represented the Romanian interests of Yakov Goldovsky. The latter had been previously convicted in Russia for asset stripping state-run enterprises.

Glencore also cut Romania-related deals with the notorious Ukrainian-Israeli Michael Cherney. Cherney has reportedly been blocked from receiving a US visa since 1999 due to alleged ties to organized crime. A diplomatic cable released by WikiLeaks and written by the US ambassador to Uzbekistan, Jon Purnell, described him as the head of a "Russian crime syndicate." It said that Cherney's brother and business partner, Lev, had traveled to Tashkent for a

2006 birthday party for a gangster known affectionately as Salim the Great. Michael sent best wishes to Salim through one of the guests, who included "Russian, Georgian, and Ukrainian criminal underworld figures, along with parliamentarians, singers, actors, and sports celebrities."

Cherney controlled a Cyprus-based company called Expanet, which bought crude oil from Glencore and resold it to a refinery in Budapest. In a 2006 letter of guarantee, Cherney thanked Glencore for "entering into, at my request, a contract with Expanet," and promised that if it failed to make payments when due, he would personally cover all debts.

Another Glencore business partner here was Romanian businessman Marian Iancu. Glencore sold him crude oil through an offshore company he controlled, Faber Invest & Trade, for processing at the RAFO refinery in Romania. Iancu was indicted for tax evasion and money laundering in 2006 and convicted in late 2011. A WikiLeaked US State Department cable described RAFO as "embroiled in a web of corruption, money laundering, fraud and criminal charges" and included Faber among its "shady entities."

Rich admitted that the old Glencore paid bribes. The new Glencore, however, denies doing so: "We will not be complicit in any third party's violation of the law in any country, nor the payment nor receipt of bribes, nor participate in any other criminal, fraudulent, or corrupt practice," reads the company's corporate practices statement.

Nonetheless, investigations over the past decade have alleged that Glencore's agents and employees made illegal payments to secure market access in a number of countries.

In 2009, US and Bahraini prosecutors investigated allegations that Glencore's employees had made $4.6 million in improper payments to executives at Aluminium Bahrain, a state-owned smelter, to secure below-market prices on aluminum products. Glencore denied the allegations; in 2009, however, it paid Aluminium Bahrain an out-of-court settlement of $20 million.

A 2008 US Senate report revealed that a client at the LGT Group, a bank owned by Liechtenstein's ruling family, discussed setting up a Panamanian shell corporation and bogus foundation to pay bribes on Glencore's behalf.

The unnamed client, an agent for the company, had an existing account at the bank that handled about $1 million annually. "A small portion of the payments go ... to the USA and Panama and may be classified as bribes," according to an internal LGT memorandum obtained by Senate investigators. The agent had set up the account in 2002; prior to then Glencore had made such payments directly, the memo said. An LGT official testified before the Senate but refused to say whether the bank had set up the Panamanian corporation or foundation at the client's request.

In 2012, a court in Belgium found that a Glencore employee bribed a European Union official for inside information that allowed it to win millions of dollars in cereal contracts. Glencore reportedly treated the official, Karel Brus, to a week's vacation at a luxury hotel on the French Riviera. Glencore also bought Brus a cell phone and picked up more than $20,000 worth of calls he made to the company, some placed just minutes before bid deadlines.

*   *   *

The frontiers are Glencore's growth engine, and nowhere more so than the Democratic Republic of the Congo, the poster child of the resource-cursed failed state. Doing business there is all but impossible without a well-connected political patron, and Glencore's partner in Kinshasa is perhaps the most wired of them all: Dan Gertler, an Israeli businessman known for his intimate ties to President Joseph Kabila.

The grandson of the founder of the Israel Diamond Exchange, Gertler turned up in Congo in 1997 at age twenty-three as the country was descending into a hellish war that left at least four million dead. Gertler had few contacts when he arrived in Congo, and a confidential report by the international investigative firm Kroll that I obtained described him as having a "poor record in fulfilling promised investments." But he did have something that a government at war desperately needed: cash. Three years after he arrived in Congo, the government—then headed by Laurent Kabila, Joseph's father, who was assassinated in 2001—sold Gertler a monopoly on diamond sales for $20 million, though it was reportedly worth hundreds of millions of dollars. Gertler denied charges of promising to provide military aid to Congo in a 2004 Israeli court case brought by Yossi Kamisa, a former Israeli antiterrorism police official who maintains that he accompanied Gertler to Congo—and even met with Laurent Kabila—to train and equip Congolese forces in exchange for diamond concessions. Gertler severed relations with Kamisa, reportedly over negative press regarding the diamonds-for-arms deals; both Kamisa's suit and a subsequent appeal were dismissed.

In Congo, Gertler's diamond monopoly became politically controversial and was canceled months after Joseph Kabila came to power. Still, he continued to land profitable deals afterward. Shimon Cohen, Gertler's London-based public relations adviser, told me that his "family trusts have invested or brought over $2 billion of investment into the mining sector" in Congo. Public records and documents released in late 2011 by a British parliamentarian show that in the previous several years the Congolese government had secretly sold vast mining assets on the cheap[8] to various British Virgin Islands–registered shell companies, several of which are linked to Gertler. "Gertler's philosophy is that everyone has a price and can be bought," the Kroll report said.

Gertler became the best-connected foreigner in Congo, enjoying "a close friendship with the president," according to Cohen. He was one of the few Westerners invited to Joseph Kabila's 2006 wedding, and, in June 2011, he joined the president on the VIP dais during Independence Day celebrations. Gertler was also extremely close to Augustin Katumba Mwanke, whom a December 2009 US diplomatic cable referred to as Kabila's "Alleged Treasurer and Enforcer." According to the cable, Katumba—who died in a plane crash in February 2012—"is viewed by many as a kind of shady, even nefarious figure within Kabila's inner circle [and] is believed to manage much of Kabila's personal fortune."

"Dan Gertler is a friend," Antoine Ghonda, a close aide to Kabila, told the *Sunday Times*, "The way our president works, he has close contacts and protects them." For his part, Gertler has called Kabila "the most promising new president in the world—a new Mandela." That's not a view shared by most observers. The US State Department's 2010 human rights report said of Kabila's Congo:

> State security forces continued to act with impunity throughout the year, committing many serious abuses, including unlawful killings, disappearances, torture, rape and engaging in arbitrary arrests and detention. Government corruption remained pervasive.

With vast mineral deposits worth an estimated $24 trillion, though, including enormous amounts of cobalt, copper, and gold, Congo has irresistible appeal to companies like Glencore, which has around $4.5 billion at stake there in three holdings. Operating in the country is simply not possible without high-level political protection, and Gertler offers it for Glencore. One former Glencore employee described the company and Gertler as "totally enmeshed" in Congo. Gertler, this person told me, "managed the entire relationship between Glencore and Kabila and the Congolese government," with Glasenberg, the CEO, flying into Kinshasa or Lubumbashi on a private jet to meet with him.

Records I examined revealed an extensive set of financial dealings between firms in which Glencore and Gertler hold significant stakes.[9] They are, for example, joint shareholders in Katanga Mining; Glencore's stake alone was worth around $2.7 billion at the time of its IPO—Glencore's fourth-largest equity holding. They both held stakes as well in Nikanor, a copper and cobalt company that Glencore provided most of the financing to purchase in exchange for exclusive rights to sell all the mineral output. (Nikanor was acquired by Katanga in January 2008 for $452 million.)

For understandable reasons, Glencore was never keen to advertise its relationship with Gertler. It did, however, offer him a series of discreet, complex, and remarkably profitable deals. In one case Glencore sold stock in Katanga Mining at roughly 60 percent of its market value to Ellesmere Global Limited, a British Virgin Islands firm whose ultimate owner was a Gertler family trust. Ellesmere quickly sold it back to Glencore at close to full market price, netting a profit of about $26 million.

In another deal a subsidiary 50 percent owned by Glencore waived its rights of first refusal to acquire an additional stake in Mutanda Mining, a copper and cobalt producer, from Gecamines, Congo's state-owned mining company. It instead recommended that the shares be sold to one of the offshore firms owned by Gertler's family trust. It's not clear why Glencore's subsidiary would have passed on the offer, because business records and documents suggest that Gertler's trust picked up the Mutanda shares for a fraction of their value.

However much Gertler made through his firms' deals with Glencore, Glencore has clearly profited too, given the huge portfolio it has accumulated in Congo. That is exactly the point. "Glencore has a Gertler everywhere," a former Glencore employee told me. "That's standard."

Indeed, Glencore doesn't partner with operators like Gertler by chance. On the contrary, it reflects the company's modus operandi: gaining access to resources through gatekeepers who have intimate connections to senior-level decision makers (and remunerating them very well, directly or indirectly, for their services). Such gatekeepers, whether agents, business partners, or the heads of service companies it uses, offer a way to navigate life on the frontier, a place where—even Glencore acknowledges—business success isn't always straightforward. As the company's IPO prospectus noted dryly, "Some of Glencore's industrial activities are located in countries where corruption is generally understood to exist." Or as a former Glencore trader told me of the company's lineup of gatekeepers, "They could do all the things I couldn't do or didn't want to do."

In Russia, Glencore's chief sponsor has been oilman Mikhail Gutseriev, who in 1995 was elected to the Duma as a member of right-wing nationalist Vladimir Zhirinovsky's party, which he also lavishly financed. Gutseriev also owned a bank and a casino, and he was running a newly created tax-free business zone in Ingushetia, a small, violence-ridden republic bordering soon-to-be war-torn Chechnya. In her book *Sale of the Century*, Chrystia Freeland described his Moscow offices as decorated in gold, crystal, and floral designs that "an eight-year-old girl with a princess fantasy and a gold credit card might concoct" and the casino's decor as "oil paintings of naked women wrapped in furs," with private bedrooms that had mirrored ceilings and Jacuzzis. "Sometimes we have special guests, and they like to be entertained," Gutseriev explained to her. Later Gutseriev went into the energy business—he was understatedly described in a US diplomatic cable released by WikiLeaks as "not known for his transparent corporate governance." He did well. He regularly appears on *Forbes*'s list of the richest Russians, with a fortune estimated in 2012 at around $6.7 billion.

A decade earlier, though, Gutseriev was down and seemingly out. In 2002, the Kremlin fired him as the head of state-owned oil firm Slavneft for resisting the company's privatization, according to the WikiLeaked cable. That same year, however, he sought to regain his position by arranging for three busloads of armed guards to take over its Moscow offices. They withdrew after occupying the building for several days, according to an account in the Russian press.

But Gutseriev soon staged a comeback. Within a few years he had bought a number of small energy firms and had patched them together into RussNeft, which by 2006 had become one of Russia's biggest oil companies. Gutseriev's meteoric rise to full-fledged oligarch status was only possible due to massive assistance from Glencore's hidden hand. Business contracts I obtained show the company financed RussNeft's "spectacular growth" and "aggressive acquisition strategy"—as one confidential 2005 Glencore document put it—at every step. Its total funding was around $2 billion, much of it funneled to offshore companies owned by Gutseriev through a Cypriot-registered company of Glencore's called Interseal.

The 2005 document said that, thanks to Glencore's financial backing, RussNeft's assets had increased fourteen times over the previous three years. Glencore had "been working closely with M. Gutseriyev since his time at Slavneft," the document said, and "appreciates his acquisitive nature and ability to identify good assets in a short space of time." A well-placed source familiar with the deals put the matter in starker terms: "Glencore associated with him because he could buy physical assets in Russia and it couldn't. The deal was sheer balls, but that's the type of thing Glencore does."

In return for its funding Glencore got an exclusive deal to market RussNeft's oil, won the right to appoint senior personnel, and ended up with about half the equity in four oil production subsidiaries. But even financial analysts have trouble figuring out RussNeft's "opaque" accounting, making it difficult to calculate Glencore's stake in the company and its subsidiaries.

Keeping oligarchs happy has been a Glencore specialty fully on display in Kazakhstan, another of those "challenging political jurisdictions" with vast energy and mineral resources. There it owns slightly more than half of Kazzinc, a huge gold, lead, and zinc producer worth up to $7.6 billion to Glencore at the time of its IPO. Glencore owns several other assets in Kazakhstan, and its gold production in the country is expected to soar, according to Deutsche Bank.

Still, Kazakhstan can be treacherous terrain for foreign investors. A US Commerce Department report warns of "burdensome regulations that often reflect a way of doing business that is reminiscent of the Soviet Union." The Heritage Foundation think tank noted similar problems in Kazakhstan: "Corruption remains endemic, eroding the rule of law."

For these reasons—and especially because major mineral

deals in Kazakhstan often need President Nazarbayev's personal approval—investors require a powerful local sponsor with close contacts to him. Glencore's is one of the best: oligarch Bulat Utemuratov, a major investor in Verny Capital, Kazzinc's second-largest shareholder (after Glencore), with a 42 percent stake.

Glencore's Kazakh partner founded ATF Bank early in the postcommunist era and became a billionaire when he sold out in 2007 to Italy's UniCredit. An old-school ex-Soviet power broker, he owns through Verny the Ritz-Carlton properties in Moscow and Vienna. Thanks to Glencore, Utemuratov, who is now Nazarbayev's special envoy to neighboring Kyrgyzstan, became far richer: Following the IPO it paid Verny $3.2 billion for its holding in Kazzinc.

Utemuratov is a former head of Kazakhstan's powerful National Security Committee who once held a top position in the ruling party and served as chief of staff to Nazarbayev between 2006 and 2008. He is known among insiders as the president's "consigliere." He is one of the few people in the country who can dependably get a meeting or phone call with Nazarbayev at any time, a Western expert on Kazakhstan told me. "You can't do any large-scale business in Kazakhstan without the president's approval, and you can't get that without direct access to the president, which Utemuratov gets for you. If you need something, you can have your CEO go over a number of times to meet with the president, and that might work, and you might get help if you can get the head of state from your home country to exert influence on him. But the most efficient and surest way to get what you need is to have support from someone local who is extremely close to Nazarbayev, and Utemuratov is one of very few people on that list."

In May 2011, a group of opposition politicians issued a public letter complaining that Kazzinc and other former state firms had been privatized under murky conditions that allowed Utemuratov and other insiders to pick up vast stakes thanks to their ties to the ruling family. Glencore could be stripped of its assets in the country, said the letter, adding, "Upon any change of regime in Kazakhstan to a democratic one, any acquisition of any shares in Kazzinc … will be subject to review."

So why did Glencore decide to go public, trading away some of that precious Swiss secrecy and opening itself to so much more scrutiny? Various theories have been floated, in addition to the obvious explanation that the move made dozens of its senior executives unimaginably rich—among them that the firm needed more capital from the markets to fuel its global growth plans, money it put to use in deals to take over giant companies, such as Xstrata.

Patrick Smith of *Africa Confidential*, who has tracked Glencore and other traders for years, thinks the move reflects a profound transition, as the old model in oil and other commodities—whereby companies and individuals built empires by leveraging relationships with top government officials—is slowly giving way to a rule-based system. Then again, Smith told me, "You can be damn sure that Glencore wouldn't have gone public if it didn't have structures in place to keep making money. It must have calculated that it can still come out ahead despite having very ambitious targets."

Even if Smith is right about the slow emergence of a more rule-based global business system, commodities trading remains as one of the world's most opaque, secretive, corrupt—and globally consequential—industries. While outright bribery has become largely passé as a business practice—due to banking restrictions on large cash movements and tighter enforcement of the US Foreign Corrupt Practices Act and similar legislation passed in Europe— traders told me that there are ever more sophisticated forms of payoffs that may skirt the spirit of antibribery laws but are often technically legal.

And will going public change Glencore notably? The company's culture goes totally against it, the former Glencore trader I interviewed in Montreux told me, especially given the strict rules and accounting practices on the London exchange. "That's just not the way traders work," he said.

Still, like all good businesses, Glencore has to keep up with the times, as even founder Marc Rich came to agree. "Discretion is an important factor of success in the commodity business," he told an interviewer when Glencore announced it would go public. "They probably don't have a choice. Transparency is requested today. It limits your activity, to be sure, but it's just a new strategy to which they have to adapt."

4

The Gatekeepers: Bretton Sciaroni

Running alongside the Mekong and Tonlé Sap rivers, the Sisowath Quay is the main drag for tourists, expatriates, and international aid workers in the Cambodian capital of Phnom Penh. By day they flock to the grounds of the Royal Palace, with its famous Silver Pagoda and dollhouse-like Napoleon III Pavilion, and to Wat Botum, a golden spire–topped Buddhist monastery (where in the 1930s a young novice monk named Saloth Sar, better known later in life as Pol Pot, was rated as "a lovely child"). At night Westerners push their way to the quay's open-air bars and restaurants through a circus of street vendors: book and video sellers, opium dealers, *tuk tuk* drivers, and the inevitable young prostitutes. ("I'm too tired these days to even think about sex," I overheard a British man complain while having a drink at a faux pub called Huxley's.) A waitress holding a small baby under her arm served them mugs of beer and the signature "Huxley's Tower" of Cajun-breaded shrimp, pork ribs, and chicken wings.

Hostess bars, the most visible component of Cambodia's notorious sex industry, are heavily clustered just off the riverfront and in a few other spots around the city. Neon lights flash from the windows, and young women sit at tables out front waving at men walking by, urging them to come in. The soundtrack trends heavily toward 1960s and '70s rock; songs like "Brown Sugar" and "Alabama Song (Whiskey Bar)" ("Show me the way / To the next little girl") are standards. Middle-aged Western men sit at tables talking to each other as hostesses drape themselves over their shoulders or in their laps, or massage their shoulders.

In his 1998 book *Off the Rails in Phnom Penh*, Amit Gilboa described Cambodia as "an anarchic festival of cheap prostitutes [where] you are never more than a few minutes away from a place to purchase sex." Prostitution isn't quite as flagrant these days, but the temporal distance from paid sex is roughly the same. Streetwalkers can be found day and night along the perimeter of Wat Phnom, the Buddhist temple that is one of Phnom Penh's top tourist sites. There are numerous karaoke bars and massage parlors, and freelance prostitutes abound at bars and nightclubs catering to Westerners.

Outside of the sex trade, though, most of Phnom Penh shuts down early. By ten o'clock the streets are free of traffic, and a motorcycle can quickly cover the city center. Along Mao Tse Tung Boulevard sit the foreign embassies and the garish blue and white tower of the antipoverty group CARE, a perfect symbol of the excesses of the international charity complex. Norodom Boulevard, named

for the country's former king, is home to the most powerful political institutions: Prime Minister Hun Sen's ruling
People's Party, whose logo, a goddess sprinkling gold
dust, is fitting for a regime whose bosses have grown rich
through corruption; and the Ministry of the Interior, which
oversees the police and otherwise maintains order.

Norodom Boulevard connects to Road Number 2, which
is lined with dozens of apparel factories and winds east
through a procession of shantytowns to the border with
Vietnam, roughly a hundred miles away. The plants, and
hundreds more around the city's periphery, have sprouted
up since 1999, when Cambodia signed a bilateral trade
agreement that for five years allowed it to export a set
quota of textiles to the United States under highly favorable terms.

Pay at local factories has remained appallingly low: One
global survey put the average wage for apparel workers
at thirty-three cents an hour, lower than anywhere but
Bangladesh.[1] Labor unions are abundant, but most are
funded and controlled by employers or the government,
and independent activists have been targeted for repression. And so even as factories poured into Cambodia and
exports boomed, apparel workers got poorer. The monthly
minimum wage at apparel plants was forty-five dollars in
2000 and a decade later it was fifty dollars; during that same
period, inflation rose by 53 percent. The low pay and poor
conditions are precisely why so many women opt to work at
hostess bars and other sex trade jobs. A labor-rights activist with a group called the Community Legal Education
Center, Tola Moeun, told me, "A lot of women no longer

want apparel jobs. When prostitution offers a better life, our factory owners need to think about more than their profit margins."[2]

The US cut most assistance to Cambodia in 1997 after Hun Sen staged a coup but resumed aid a decade later. Today Cambodia is the third-largest recipient of US aid in Southeast Asia, after Indonesia and the Philippines. Competition with China for influence in the region and growing trade ties—the United States buys more than half of Cambodia's apparel production, its primary export—are among the factors behind the political warming.

But a US diplomatic cable written in 2007 and released by WikiLeaks pointed to another reason for the rapprochement: the discovery of massive extractable resources, including gold, bauxite, and other minerals, plus potentially large reserves of oil and gas.

Doing business in Cambodia is not easy, though. The WikiLeaks cable said corruption in the country was "systemic and pervasive" and expressed concern that Cambodia might become "the Nigeria of Southeast Asia." One Western investor I talked to described the situation as "a nightmare," saying, "Anything having to do with licenses, natural resources, or concessions—that's where you have problems and where you always have military and government officials looking for money."

For major Western companies trying to navigate this complicated and perilous investment climate, this is where Bretton Sciaroni comes in. The portly Sciaroni makes a most unusual power broker in contemporary

Cambodia. A former ideologue of Ronald Reagan's White House, he played a little-known but vital role in enabling Oliver North's weapons shipments and assistance to the Nicaraguan Contras during the 1980s. Yet now he is an official adviser to the government of Prime Minister Hun Sen, a one-time Khmer Rouge cadre. The Cambodian government has bestowed upon Sciaroni the titles of minister without portfolio and his excellency. He is the chairman of the International Business Chamber (IBC), an association that includes most of the multinational corporations in Cambodia and which is the most important business group in the country.

From his office in an exclusive section of the city—his neighbors include the president of the ruling party—he runs a consulting firm, Sciaroni & Associates, which provides advice and counsel to foreign investors seeking to do business in Cambodia. He has brokered land and natural resource deals that offer little to the public but that benefit government officials and well-connected domestic and foreign insiders, including Bretton Sciaroni.

Sciaroni's clients include a number of natural resource firms, including Chevron, which received a stake in the most promising field. "Of particular importance for an investor in an emerging economy is the establishment and maintenance of good government relations," his firm's Web site explains of its modus operandi.

> Sciaroni & Associates enjoys excellent working relationships with major ministries and governmental institutions. Several of our senior staff have served or are serving in various official capacities

with the [Cambodian government], giving them the understanding of both the people and processes of government.

Unlike international oil fixers, who often have global ambitions and influence, Sciaroni is a gatekeeper whose utility is limited to Cambodia and a few neighboring countries. His skill set is also narrower, and is based almost exclusively on his ability to leverage his political contacts to open doors. For example, Sciaroni worked with a company called Raptor Forestry, which was (according to a confidential business plan) exploring large-scale agricultural and forestry projects. "The compelling nature of this opportunity is the ability of the project to return investors' funds within 12–18 months," the proposal said. "Assuming assumptions are met, investors can expect a ... continuing share in an estimated $35 million in free cash from clearing activities." Sciaroni, it said, had been given an equity stake for providing his "network of local contacts and delivering legal services to the project."

The gatekeeper role is frequently played by well-connected locals and is especially common in countries where the rule of law is weak and corruption is especially entrenched. In Cambodia, Sciaroni is one of a handful of foreigners who arrived in the country during the chaos of the post–Khmer Rouge period and who have lived well and amassed influence through their dedication to the new leadership. Among them are Helen Jarvis, an Australian academic who became an adviser to Sok An, the country's deputy prime minister.

Sciaroni is the most influential of the foreign lot. The

others have curried favor through ideological fealty and support for Hun Sen's regime—"They are more pro-government than the government," one source told me. Sciaroni has done that as well, but he has also played a hugely important role with his consulting firm. And unlike the other prominent foreigners, who are recognized as progovernment hacks by Western diplomats, Sciaroni has managed in large measure to avoid that taint. He consults regularly with the US and British embassies and is viewed as an important interlocutor. The US embassy in Phnom Penh selected Sciaroni to represent Cambodia at a Global Business Conference hosted by Secretary of State Hillary Clinton in Washington in early 2012. In August of that year he hosted an event at his law firm to welcome the new American ambassador, William Todd.

During a reporting trip to Cambodia in 2011, I met Sciaroni for drinks at the Elephant Bar of the Raffles Hotel. Sciaroni wore a light-colored jacket and yellow tie and sported gold-rimmed glasses and a thick gold bracelet; he offered an upbeat view of his adopted country. "This is very much an emerging economy and democracy," he said, while sipping from a glass of Château Batailley, a French Bordeaux. "There's been a lot of political progress. The ruling party no longer intimidates the opposition." He describes his own work in Cambodia in an altruistic fashion, saying, "This is a country where you can make a difference. If you make a suggestion to a government official, and he likes it, it will happen."

Dana Rohrabacher, a conservative California congress-man and old friend of Sciaroni's, takes a dimmer view of his work there and relationship with the regime. Though he says he personally likes Sciaroni, Rohrabacher told me that Hun Sen—who has held power since the 1997 coup— "had no genuine legitimacy" and that "Brett has become part and parcel of a clique of the Cambodian elite that is neither democratic nor honest."

How did a fervent right-wing anticommunist and old pal of Ollie North's end up in Cambodia as the chief foreign advocate for Hun Sen, a man who in the 1960s fought as a Khmer Rouge guerrilla against a US-backed government before becoming head of the Vietnamese puppet regime that overthrew Pol Pot in 1979? It was a big ideological leap, but Sciaroni's chief talent—performing intellectual acrobatics for his paymasters, whoever they might be—has served him equally well in Washington and Phnom Penh.

By 1984, just five years after he received a law degree from UCLA, the sky seemed the limit for young Bretton Sciaroni. Following short stints at two right-wing think tanks and as a Commerce Department political appointee under President Reagan, he was named chief counsel to the president's Intelligence Oversight Board. During this period he provided the legal arguments Reagan needed to move forward with his Star Wars scheme (on the specious grounds that it didn't violate the Anti-Ballistic Missile Treaty) and with military aid to the Nicaraguan Contras, which Congress had flatly forbidden.

When Iran–Contra investigators subsequently asked him why the administration turned to him for advice instead of to more experienced staff lawyers at the White

House or Justice Department, Sciaroni replied, "Frankly … that thought has crossed my mind as well. I don't know why my opinion was the only one."

The reason, however, was quite apparent. Like John Yoo and other conservatives on whom the Bush administration more recently relied for the flimflam needed to justify torturing terrorism suspects in violation of the Geneva Conventions, Sciaroni was a loyalist who the Reagan administration knew would reach the conclusions it wanted.

Indeed, compared with Sciaroni, Yoo looks like Oliver Wendell Holmes. In 1986, Sciaroni wrote a series of opinions, including a memo that said North's aid to the Contras was legal even though Congress, through the so-called Boland Amendment, had flatly banned any training "that amounts to participation in the planning or execution of military or paramilitary operations in Nicaragua." Sciaroni determined that the Boland Amendment ban didn't cover "generic" military aid, which he expansively defined to include categories such as marksmanship, intelligence reporting, and the construction of fortifications.

When he was later asked by a superior at the oversight board to investigate media accounts of illegal aid to the Contras, Sciaroni determined that they were false, largely on the basis of a five-minute conversation with North. The latter denied everything, which was good enough for Sciaroni.

Lou Cannon, Ronald Reagan's biographer, later wrote that the Reagan administration's claim that it could arm the Contras despite the Boland Amendment was an after-the-fact invention constructed to provide a legal rationale for North and others ... who were charged with violating the law. If the Reagan administration had questioned the legality of Boland, it could have and should have challenged the issue in the courts. What happened instead was that the law was evaded while the president and his surrogates were proclaiming that it was being obeyed.

Sciaroni's 1987 testimony before the congressional committee investigating Iran–Contra was a disaster for the Reagan administration (and would have been even worse had it not been overshadowed in the media by the appearance on the stand the same day of Fawn Hall, Oliver North's attractive secretary). During his testimony it emerged that he only passed the bar exam on his fourth try—in three states—and that he was given the chief counsel's position despite never having previously held a job in the legal profession.

> CONGRESSMAN THOMAS FOLEY: Were you ever involved in writing legal opinions on legislative acts prior to your service with the board?
>
> SCIARONI: I can't recall that I was.
>
> FOLEY: Did you ever write one before the September 1985 opinion that you've described?
>
> SCIARONI: None comes to mind.
>
> FOLEY: So this is the first time in your legal career that you ever wrote an opinion regarding a legislative act?
>
> SCIARONI: Perhaps outside law school.

Sciaroni was dismissed from his government job soon after his testimony. In early 1988, a group of right-wing supporters held a fundraiser at Washington's prestigious University Club to help pay the lawyers he'd hired to help him prepare for his questioning. In an interview at the fundraiser with the *Washington Post*, Sciaroni was clearly feeling sorry for himself. "Congress writes a bad law," he said. "I write an opinion, which is correct. I get roasted on national television ... It is so blatantly unfair."

The following years were rough for Sciaroni. He surfaced in 1991 as a fellow at the American Conservative Union and the same year became a pro bono lobbyist for an outfit called the Central America Lawyers Group (CALG), which was registered at a Miami post office box. In disclosure forms, Sciaroni described the lawyers (none of whom were identified) as dedicated to "creating a just society in El Salvador."

The CALG was actually a front for the murderous right-wing Salvadoran government, which was prosecuting a civil war against leftist guerrillas. Its chief mission was to whitewash the military's appalling human rights record, specifically the notorious murder of six Jesuits in 1989. The following year a task force led by Congressman Joe Moakley issued a report that said the two soldiers convicted of the killings in Salvadoran courts were fall guys for the true culprits, a group of senior Salvadoran officers. The report said that one of the key figures who ordered the killings was Colonel René Emilio Ponce, who had been promoted to minister of defense in late 1990 and was a close ally of the Reagan administration. Moakley said at the time:

> From the beginning, our task force was asked to view the murders of the Jesuits as the deranged actions of a few individuals, and not as an indictment of the armed forces as an institution. It is my view that it is both.

The Moakley report was a PR catastrophe for the Salvadoran regime and threatened to lead to the end of American aid to the country, which Congress had already cut in half. In response, the CALG produced a 150-page booklet that it used to lobby Congress, deriding Moakley's report as a "conspiracy theory." The study, which thanked the Salvadoran government and military, was clearly written by Sciaroni and demonstrated the same intellectual dexterity he deployed on behalf of the Contras. While Moakley alleged that there was a high-level plot to kill the Jesuits, the CALG said that there was "no evidence of any specific orders, general policy, or permissive environment fostered by the High Command demonstrating institutional guilt." There was also no evidence that Ponce had anything to do with the murders; indeed, he had "actively assisted investigators." The Salvadoran government and military cooperated with investigators and never sought to control or influence the investigation. "As important as the successful resolution of the Jesuit case is, its outcome—whatever it may be—should not effect fundamental US–Salvadoran relations," CALG argued.[3]

Two years later a United Nations truth commission issued a report that corroborated Moakley's findings and demolished the claims of CALG and the right-wing government. Reinaldo Figueredo, one of the commissioners, said at the time:

In examining the staggering breadth of the violence that occurred in El Salvador, the Commission was moved by the senselessness of the killings, the brutality with which they were committed, the terror that they created in the people, in other words the madness, or locura, of the war.

Nonetheless, American aid to the Salvadoran regime was never cut off, just as Sciaroni and the CALG hoped.[4]

By 1993, Sciaroni's career prospects in Washington were grim. That year he learned from Congressman Rohrabacher that Hun Sen was looking to hire an American attorney for a short-term assignment. Sciaroni was quick to seize the opportunity. He arrived right before the May 1993 elections, which were organized by the UN following the reign of the Khmer Rouge and years of civil war. The royalist party triumphed in the balloting but agreed to a power-sharing arrangement when Hun Sen and his Cambodian People's Party (CPP), which came in a distant second, threatened to lead an armed revolt.

"Pol Pot killed all the [Cambodian] lawyers," Sciaroni told me at the Elephant Bar, in explaining his good luck in getting the job. "They had some French ones, but I think they wanted an American ... Rohrabacher came to me and said, 'How would you like to go to Cambodia for two months?' The funny thing is that if the CPP had won the election, I probably would have been back in the US after two months. But they lost, and they panicked. I had written up some things they liked, and they asked me to stay on."

Rohrabacher has been a strong critic of Hun Sen ever since the 1993 vote, so it seemed odd that he would help Sciaroni get a job with the CPP, but the congressman confirmed the story during a phone conversation. It turned out that Rohrabacher and Sciaroni had known each other since their college days, when they were members of Young Americans for Freedom and Youth for Reagan. "After the Iran–Contra scandal, all of Brett's friends deserted him, which is typical of Washington," Rohrabacher told me. "A Cambodian–American constituent told me that Hun Sen was going to hold free elections; he was looking for a lawyer to draw up an honest election code and was willing to pay top dollar. I knew Brett really needed the money and thought he'd be perfect for the job. And he did a good job—they did have a free and fair first-round vote. The only problem was that Hun Sen lost and didn't abide by the results, and our government buckled. They should have told him, 'You lost, get out,' but instead they agreed to a compromise, and Hun Sen became one of the two prime ministers."

Rohrabacher was furious about the outcome, but Sciaroni continued to work for Hun Sen.

"He's like a *Lord Jim* character," Rohrabacher told me of Sciaroni. "His own country abandoned him when Iran–Contra became a scandal. He became a destroyed human being who went overseas to start a new life."

Sciaroni's close relationship with the regime became especially apparent after Hun Sen seized power in a bloody military coup in July 1997 that left at least forty-one oppositionists dead. At his government's request, Sciaroni assembled and directed a lobbying and public relations team that tried to spin the coup in Washington. The center-piece of the campaign was a "white paper" that alleged that the royalist party had employed a "campaign of provoca-tion" against the CPP, and that the coup was therefore a legitimate preemptive measure by Hun Sen.

The *Washington Times* exposed the campaign, prompt-ing outrage among Americans in Cambodia and some of Sciaroni's right-wing comrades back home. "In private conversations, members of the American community in Phnom Penh have expressed outrage over Mr. Sciaroni's role in helping create the legal defense," the newspaper said. "Other lawyers, upset at the way Hun Sen crushed his rival, said they would have refused to do so on ethical grounds." When the *Times* asked him what help or advice he contributed to the white paper, "Sciaroni grimaced and responded, 'No comment.'"

In 1998, Sciaroni coordinated another PR campaign around an election that Hun Sen organized and won handily. The International Republican Institute, an organization with ties to the Republican Party, described the election as "among the worst we have observed" and "fundamentally flawed." Problems it pointed to included the forced exile of opposition leaders after the 1997 coup, the "destruction of opposition party infrastructures," the denial of media access to opposition parties, and "the murder of up to 100 opposition members without any resolution to the crimes."

Rita Colorito, who worked on the campaign for an American lobbying firm recruited by Sciaroni, later wrote about her experience in an article called "Confessions of a Spin Doctor." "The Cambodian People's Party didn't care about human rights progress," she wrote. "It simply wanted favorable media coverage and renewed international aid."

Hun Sen's American spin team did its best to sell their client by "taking semantics to an absurdity," according to Colorito:

> We argued incessantly that only Hun Sen could deal with the lingering threat [of the Khmer Rouge]. Although he had driven the regime from Phnom Penh in 1978—with the help of the Vietnamese army—we ignored the fact that he'd once been a Khmer Rouge lieutenant. More important, as of June 1998, the Khmer Rouge amounted to some 400 ill-equipped guerrillas in Cambodia's far northern jungles. Yet, our campaign mantra focused on this vastly exaggerated fear ...
>
> After the elections, the Cambodian Ambassador asked me directly how we could make the media like them. "You can't just say you'll investigate killings, you actually have to do it," I explained, referring to the 100 opposition supporters that had been killed since the 1997 coup.
>
> The Washington team advised they investigate at least one killing to demonstrate progress. We suggested Thong Sophal, whom Cambodian police claimed had committed suicide. Sophal's eyes had been gouged out, his arms and legs cut off, and his body skinned. The ambassador looked at me blankly, then uttered the standard refrain: "It's not easy. It will take one, maybe two years."

Sciaroni's campaign misfired, though, when it persuaded Tina Rosenberg of the *New York Times Magazine* to come to Cambodia to report on Hun Sen's inspired leadership. Rosenberg wasn't impressed and wrote an article (under the headline "Hun Sen Stages an Election") that said that since 1975 "Cambodia has suffered under an assortment of dreadful Governments, and Hun Sen has been in all of them."

Petrified that Rosenberg's story would cause them to lose their fat contract, the PR team held an "emergency phone conference" to spin the article to Hun Sen and convince him that it wasn't as bad as it looked. Hun Sen apparently accepted the explanation. Sciaroni continued to enjoy a close relationship with his government, and in 2002 it granted him Cambodian citizenship.

Sciaroni's success is based on a simple truth. Political contacts are the handmaiden of business operations the world over, but in a country like Cambodia—with its tiny intertwined political and economic elite—they are vital. "You get opportunities because you are close to the government," a Western diplomat told me over coffee in Phnom Penh. "You have to be in their good graces. You can accumulate wealth and live comfortably but to accumulate jet-set wealth requires government connections."

No critic of the CPP would ever be allowed to develop a major business, he said, because that would allow him or her to gain financial resources and public prominence, and ultimately challenge the regime. "Economic development tends to be land intensive, which is all concession-based," he said. "That totally depends on your relationship with the government. What are the chances you will be able to do business if you criticize it? Zero."

Sciaroni's connections, this person said, run wide and deep: "Brett has been here since the early days, when things were very rough. There aren't many [foreigners like that], and Brett is the only American."

Sciaroni is well known in Phnom Penh and is a fixture at Freebird, which offers "The Best American Food in Cambodia." The restaurant's walls are covered with pictures of Elvis Presley, Marilyn Monroe, and Bob Denver and Alan Hale (better known as Gilligan and the Skipper), and typical menu entrées include a cheeseburger, rib-eye steak, and meatloaf and mashed potatoes.

Sciaroni founded his consulting firm in 1993, the year he arrived in the country. His chief partner at Sciaroni & Associates is Matthew Nicholas Rendall, an Australian attorney described by *Fortune* magazine as the leading land attorney in Cambodia. A BBC story called him "the land lawyer, in a sharp suit, who advised the government so closely that it is often said that he 'wrote' Cambodia's investor-friendly 2001 Land Law."

The firm's Web site says that Cambodian laws and regulations "often are vague or so general as to preclude obvious application in specific circumstance," and that, as a result, governmental officials "frequently have discretion in interpretation and implementation." Sciaroni & Associates has long "worked at maintaining a good relationship with key officials in the major ministries," it continues. "This relationship is important not only to better understand governmental policies but also to work toward mutually advantageous interpretations of vague or general laws." The Web site even boasts a testimonial from Hun Sen, who congratulates "his Excellency Bretton" for "seeking justice for Khmers" and expresses hope that "he will continue to stay here with us."

Everyone from Amnesty International to Freedom House has condemned Cambodia's human rights record. The State Department's 2011 annual report on human rights said that Hun Sen's ruling CPP has "consolidated control of the three branches of government and other national institutions" and that the government "restricted freedom of speech and of the press ... and at times interfered with freedom of assembly."

Sciaroni, needless to say, has quite a different assessment. "Investor confidence has been strengthened by the awareness of political stability," he said during a speech at a 2007 investment conference.

> From one mandate to another, you are likely to deal with the same ministers in the last mandate that you deal with in the next mandate, and very likely the next mandate. You don't have the revolving door phenomenon that other [Third World countries] have. Therefore you are not likely to see great swings in policy because of new officials coming on the scene.

In other words, Hun Sen's authoritarian brand of government is a plus for business.

He also has sought to minimize human rights violations and kindred abuses. In an op-ed for the *Phnom Penh Post*, he chided the World Bank's resident country director for warning that the "incarceration of political figures could affect Cambodia's ability to attract investors." In fact, said Sciaroni, the "protection of free speech when that speech is irresponsibly exercised" was a far bigger concern. By his reckoning, opposition protests of the bogus 1998 election—that he was paid to spin as a great democratic moment—amounted to an example of such irresponsible free speech.

Son Chhay, one of the few oppositionists in Parliament, said he feared Sciaroni had played a role in softening American policy toward Cambodia, which until a few years ago placed a heavy emphasis, at least rhetorically, on human rights. Nowadays, expanded trade and military cooperation get far higher billing. Sciaroni "covers up the government's bad practices and uses his connections to convince the US to keep [supporting] the government," he told me. Another government critic, who asked to remain unidentified, offered a similar assessment. The United States has become "obsessed with the need for 'dialogue' with the government, and Sciaroni is seen as a bridge for that," this person said.

Sciaroni is not shy about what he can deliver for clients of his consulting firm. During a speech at a conference for foreign investors in Phnom Penh he explained how his firm had negotiated a deal for an American company that had balked at investing locally because the import of raw aluminum was taxed at a rate of 7 percent. "In rapid succession we met various senior officials," Sciaroni recounted. "[One of them] said 'what would you like it [the rate] to be?' and the company said 'How about zero percent?' And zero percent it was and is today."

The Sciaroni & Associates Web site says the list of its clients comes "from various sectors and includes global blue chip giants as well as leading regional companies." One of its specialties is negotiating deals for natural resources firms, especially mining and energy firms. The company "has provided advice to the majority of extractive industry companies in the Royal Kingdom of Cambodia for many years," says the Web site. The head of Sciaroni & Associates natural resources practice, Billie Jean Slott, is the cofounder and legal adviser to the Cambodian Association for Mining and Exploration Companies.

The natural resources industry has been a cash cow for Hun Sen and his ruling party. "A corrupt elite has captured the country's emerging oil and mineral sectors," Global Witness said in a 2009 report called "Country for Sale." It said Cambodia could earn vast wealth from oil and minerals, but that its "future is being jeopardized by high-level corruption, nepotism, and patronage in the allocation and management of these critical public assets." According to Global Witness, key concessions and resources were awarded "behind closed doors" by a few power brokers with close ties to Prime Minister Hun Sen and senior government officials.

A number of Sciaroni's clients have obtained concessions in Cambodia through murky means. For example, clients at his consulting firm include Chevron, which won stakes in Cambodia's most promising oil field. Production has been delayed, but Chevron originally estimated its holdings in the Gulf of Thailand at four hundred million barrels, enough to generate peak annual earnings of about

$1.7 billion a year. Chevron was one of seventy-five oil, gas, and mining firms that refused to reveal how much they paid for their stakes in Cambodia, making it impossible to track whether the money ended up in the national treasury or the pockets of regime officials.

Another Sciaroni client, BHP Billiton, an Australian firm that won a bauxite project in Cambodia, was alleged to have paid a $2.5 million bribe to close its deal, according to published accounts and the parliamentarian Son Chhay. The payment, which was supposed to go to a social fund to develop projects for local communities, disappeared into a black hole and never found its way into government books. As a result, not a single school, hospital, or irrigation project was built by the fund, as had been pledged by both BHP and the government.

"No doubt BHP knew from the beginning this money [was a] bribe," Son Chhay told an Australian newspaper. "There is no excuse for BHP."[5]

That Sciaroni's clients have been accused of making suspicious payments to the Cambodian government does not, of course, mean that they did so at his suggestion nor is there any evidence to suggest that. What it does show is the difficulty of doing business in a country where corruption is so rife. Indeed, while Sciaroni has been a public apologist for the government's record on human rights and good government, in private he has acknowledged that corruption is a major problem. "Cambodia currently has laws which criminalize corruption-related offenses, including extortion and bribery," he is quoted as saying in a 2009 US government cable released by WikiLeaks. But Sciaroni, the cable said, noted that the political will to enforce these provisions is lacking, as evidenced by a dearth of corruption-related prosecutions. He warned against allowing the lack of prosecutions to lull business people into a false sense of immunity and an acceptance that corrupt practices are business as usual.

Sciaroni's consulting firm has also been involved in shaping Cambodian land law and in brokering land deals that have benefited his clients and Sciaroni personally. I spent two days in Sihanoukville, a seedy but gorgeous coastal town whose beaches and islands have been sold off by the government to well-connected domestic and foreign companies that said they were planning eco-friendly luxury hotel and condominium projects. All of this was done by decree, without public disclosure, and with the terms of the deals kept secret. "Those who lived or worked there were turfed out—some jailed, others beaten, virtually all denied meaningful compensation," said a 2008 story in the *Guardian*. The newspaper quoted a British property developer, Marty Kaye, who said, "Nowhere else in the world could you create your own kingdom from scratch ... It's fantastically exciting, the opportunity to zone [a] whole island, to see where the luxury exclusive villa plots will be, for the Brad Pitts, etc."

By now, almost all of Cambodia's coast is owned privately, by rich locals and foreigners. According to the *Guardian*, "The Sokha Hotel Group, run by Sok Kong, a Cambodian oligarch and Hun Sen ally, was confirmed as the new owner of the lion's share of Occheuteal Beach, the largest and most popular public dune in the region." Kith Meng, another businessman with close ties to the ruling party and a personal adviser to Hun Sen, obtained beautiful islands and property in the region. A WikiLeaked cable from 2007 called Kit Meng "Mr. Rough Stuff" and quoted sources who described him as "a relatively young and ruthless gangster" who was "notorious for using his bodyguards to coerce others into brokering deals."

A number of well-connected foreigners landed deals during the Sihanoukville sell-off as well. The *Guardian* reported:

> With all the big islands sold, even smaller outcrops have gone, too, including a clump of rocks known as Nail Island, bought by Ukrainian entrepreneur Nickolai Doroshenko, who has transformed it into a James Bond–style lair, complete with a giant fibre-glass shark that soars over the fortress-like construction. He already owns Victory Beach, in Sihanoukville, a restaurant stuffed with live snakes and a bar that advertises "swimming girls."

Sciaroni was listed on initial incorporation records as chairman of the board of a local subsidiary of Paris-based CityStar, another consulting firm client for which he also provides legal counsel. CityStar set up shop in Cambodia in early 2007, almost precisely as the government was selling off for development public land near the coastal town of Sihanoukville. CityStar quickly won two concessions in Ream National Park, which contains beaches, mangrove forests, jungle, and, according to a UN Web site of protected areas, 150 species of birds and a noted monkey population—as well as two areas for development on islands off the coast of Sihanoukville.

"Our development will be really green and in total accordance with landscapes and vegetations," Etienne Chenevier, CityStar's executive director in Asia, told the local press. "We will have very low density villas or cluster villas, a few bungalow hotels with everything … in respect with the Cambodian spirit." He said the selling price of villas would range between $170,000 and $200,000, and he expected buyers from Phnom Penh and France.

A foreign businessman I spoke with in Phnom Penh said that Cambodia had great potential but corruption and the government's lack of concern for the poor—the overwhelming majority of the population—were holding the country back. "To get to the next level, like elsewhere in Asia, they need a healthy, educated population," he told me during an interview at his office. "Vietnam and Laos have done better with rural electrification and educating their people. I can't believe I'm saying this sort of thing, because I'm generally right-wing, but you have to have schools and health care to make your economy run better, and the private sector is just not going to do it."

My visit took place during the early days of the Arab Spring, and the businessman said that the uprisings in the Middle East made him wonder about Cambodia's political stability. "People ask if a Libya or Egypt could happen here and I wonder. You have the same conditions here as forty years ago—a wealthy and corrupt elite in Phnom Penh and the Average Joe is very poor. The prime minister has consolidated power. The risk is that they get too greedy."

As for political reform, he added, "We may never see real democracy here. Strong, authoritarian leaders have always been the types that do well in this region."

But for now the future looks bright in Cambodia—at least for the ruling party and hangers-on like Sciaroni.[6] American companies like GE, DuPont, and Microsoft have set up shop here in recent years, and his firm recently began offering "the same experienced advice for clients with business interests in Myanmar and Laos."

Cambodia's ties to the US government are also warming. Then secretary of state Hillary Clinton traveled there on an official visit in 2012, and Barack Obama visited the same year to attend the East Asia Summit. His aides claimed that he pressed Hun Sen in private on political freedoms, but in public he didn't raise the subject of human rights abuses and pointedly declined to meet with opposition political figures or activists. Following the visit, Sciaroni told the local press that relations between the United States and Cambodia had never been better. "This goes beyond the business relationships: diplomatic, political, economic relations are all very good between Cambodia and the United States," he said.

And so it goes for Bretton Sciaroni, whose fleeting success in Ronald Reagan's Washington served as a stepping-stone for far bigger things here. "Opportunities abound," he told me of Cambodia when we met for drinks, though he may as well have been describing his own good fortune in washing up here. "It's a great environment."

5

The Flacks: Tony Blair

Vast oil reserves and geographic proximity to Afghanistan have made Kazakhstan an important Western energy and military ally in the past decade, but few observers have any illusions about its corrupt, despotic ruler. President Nursultan Nazarbayev has led the country since it became independent of the Soviet Union, and in 2011 he was reelected in a rigged balloting with 95 percent of the vote. A rubber-stamp legislature has exempted him from a constitutional two-term presidential term limit, which effectively makes him president for life. Nazarbayev has been granted the permanent right "to address the people of Kazakhstan at any time" and to approve all "initiatives on the country's development," according to a US State Department account.

The WikiLeaks release of US diplomatic cables in 2010 comically undermined the sober public images cultivated by the Kazakh ruling elite. One waggish dispatch called "Lifestyles of the Kazakhstani Leadership" begins by dryly recounting that political leaders in the former Soviet republic "appear to enjoy typical hobbies—such as travel, horseback riding, and skiing." But then the cable goes on to observe that the country's oil-besotted leaders "are able to indulge in their hobbies on a grand scale, whether flying Elton John to Kazakhstan for a concert or trading domestic property for a palace in the United Arab Emirates." As a representative study, the cable notes that in 2007:

> President Nazarbayev's son-in-law, Timur Kulibayev, celebrated his 41st birthday in grand style. At a small venue in Almaty, he hosted a private concert with some of Russia's biggest pop-stars. The headliner, however, was Elton John, to whom he reportedly paid one million pounds for this one-time appearance. (Note: The British Ambassador relayed a slightly different story, with an unknown but obviously well-heeled friend arranging and paying for Sir Elton's gig.)

Kazakhstan sits at the heart of the Caspian Sea region, in Central Asia, and the WikiLeaks cables paint the same rough portrait of other energy-rich nations of the region. In one diplomatic missive, a US diplomat compares Azerbaijani president Ilham Aliyev to Sonny Corleone. Like Don Vito's kid, Aliyev was prone to overreact when he perceived challenges "to his authority or affronts to his family dignity, even minor ones," said a 2009 cable, in a reference to the president's tendency to lock up critics and shut down newspapers. As the dispatch explained, "He typically devises [foreign policy] with pragmatism, restraint and a helpful bias toward integration with the West, yet at home his policies have become increasingly authoritarian and hostile to diversity of political views." Another WikiLeaked cable from January 2010 said that observers in Baku, the capital,

> often note that today's Azerbaijan is run in a manner similar to the feudalism found in Europe during the Middle Ages: a handful of well-connected families control certain geographic areas, as well as certain sectors of the economy ... As a result, an economy already burgeoning with oil and gas revenues produces enormous opportunity and wealth for a small handful of players that form Azerbaijan's elite.

In a series of cables on the most influential families in Azerbaijan—titled, with refreshing candor, "Azerbaijan: Who Owns What?"—an embassy hand notes that the country's first lady has managed a sort of trifecta in phony civic achievement: Mehriban Aliyeva, née Pashayeva, "besides being the wife of the President, is a Member of Parliament[1] and head of the Heydar Aliyev Foundation, a nontransparent organization that bills itself as a vehicle for charitable works." The cables closely examined the economic power of Aliyeva, whose family has vast interests in banking, insurance, construction, telecommunications, and real estate, not to mention owning Baku's first and only Bentley dealership.

Things get less decorous from there. "The Pashayev women are known to be fashion-conscious and daring, far more so than the average woman in majority-Muslim

Azerbaijan," we learn. And then, with the word-mincing prelude out of the way:

> Mehriban Aliyeva appears to have had substantial cosmetic surgery, presumably overseas, and wears dresses that would be considered provocative even in the Western world … On television, in photos, and in person, she appears unable to show a full range of facial expression.

The first lady's reconstructive work also created an issue of some delicacy when second lady Lynne Cheney arrived for a state dinner in September 2008. Flanked by her two daughters, Aliyeva didn't immediately present herself as the matron of the trio, so the crack embassy staff had to make some quick calculations in order to tell the Secret Service whom to introduce to whom. "Emboffs"—embassy officials, in cable jargon—"and White House staff studied the three for several moments, and then Emboff said, 'Well, logically the mother would probably stand in the middle.' "

There are also various illuminating cables from Uzbekistan, another former Soviet republic now run by an autocratic clan. One cable from 2005 recounts the story of a powerful first daughter who is looking to burnish her public image. The Uzbek press, the cable writer informs us, has lately run an "unusual series of articles promoting the virtue and selflessness of Gulnara Karimova," who is said to harbor ambitions of succeeding her father (perhaps best known internationally for gunning down and periodically boiling alive his political opponents).

But the strategy doesn't seem to be taking. "Most Uzbeks

see Karimova as a greedy, power-hungry individual who uses her father to crush business people or anyone else who stands in her way," said the cable writer. In one interview with an Uzbek paper, the dispatch continued, Karimova portrayed herself as "a highly principled person who listens to her conscience [and] went so far as to say that people treat you the way you treat them, and if you don't treat others well, you will 'find yourself in a blind alley.'" The correspondent then archly noted: "The many people crushed by Karimova would likely relish the chance to catch her blind in an alley." Even with the press campaign to improve her image, Karimova's "charm offensive will not likely make her more popular; she remains the single most hated person in the country. (Comment: We have no polling data to support that statement, but we stand by it. End comment.)"[2]

Nor do the subtler protocols of a foreign political order escape the discerning eye of a properly trained US embassy official. In the staggeringly grim republic of Turkmenistan, one cable notes somewhat ruefully that given the rampant state of official bribery in the capital city of Ashgabat, "US anti-corruption laws [add] a new layer of complexity and uncertainty for US firms wishing to do business here." Another Wikileaked dispatch, meanwhile, handicaps the prospects for enhancing public trust under the rule of President Gurbanguly Berdimuhamedov as dim indeed. "Berdimuhamedov does not like people who are smarter than he is," this cable writer relates. "Since he's not a very bright guy, our source offered, he is suspicious of a lot of people."

Despite this dark landscape, Caspian rulers have had few problems lining up support in Washington. "The oil and gas reserves of … Caspian littoral states can ensure the energy needs of the entire world within the next 200 years," Ali Hasanov, a senior Azeri official, said in 2012. Hasanov was surely overstating the case—that year the Caspian produced only 3.4 percent of global oil supply and Saudi Arabia alone has more proven oil reserves—but there's no doubt about the region's growing importance as a global energy supplier.

Like other corrupt, ruthless foreign regimes, Caspian leaders have hired up numerous lobbying and PR firms to peddle themselves to the American public and policy makers. But lobbying is subject to disclosure laws, and hence in recent years foreign governments and interests seeking influence in Washington have increasingly turned to other means, which are largely unregulated and don't always require public disclosure. These include: making contributions to think tanks, universities, and nonprofit groups; setting up business associations that advocate for better political ties with the US but aren't legally defined as lobbying organizations; and offering huge consulting contracts and speaking fees to politically prominent Westerners. These financial flows have helped recruit many prominent Western cheerleaders, including retired politicians (and their offspring), corporate titans, college professors, think-tank fellows, and countless former senior government officials, who use their experience and connections to promote the oil industry's interests in these countries and advocate for closer ties to the US.

Few have donned the pom-poms with as much vigor, or made as much money, as former British prime minister Tony Blair, whose work in Central Asia is just a small component of the burgeoning business realm he's built since resigning from public office in 2007. Blair moved to cash in on his time as prime minister almost immediately upon departing from Downing Street. Records on file at the Advisory Committee on Business Appointments (ACOBA), a British government agency, show that he signed on with the Washington Speakers Bureau in October 2007, four months after he stepped down, reportedly netting a $600,000 signing bonus. The records show that he gave his first paid speech that same month, though whom he addressed is not disclosed.

Blair is available to speak on any of sixteen topics, ranging from the global economy and human rights to emerging markets and overcoming obstacles and challenges, and generally "offers an unparalleled analysis of the world's most difficult and complex issues." Unlike the case with most speakers represented by the bureau, no information is provided about what it costs to hear Blair provide his pearls of wisdom. The Web site says only that fees "vary based on location and inquiries should be made to the WSB."

But one can get a sense of his standard fee by consulting the Web site of the All American Speakers Bureau, another agency that at one time represented Blair (and which still advertises his services). All American puts Blair in its category of Celebrity Headliners and pegs his minimum fee as $200,000. That's twice the rate demanded by Donald Trump, four times higher than for comedian Don Rickles and ten times higher than for Leah "Coco" Fort, "the developer of the four-step process to personal success known as the Coco Conversion."

In December 2008, he established Tony Blair Associates (TBA), "which will allow him to provide, in partnership with others, strategic advice on both a commercial and pro bono basis, on political and economic trends and governmental reform." Through TBA, Blair uses his Rolodex to provide door opening services to clients, and also takes a cut on future deals. It's not entirely clear what he does in exchange for the stiff fees he receives. A 2009 story in *New York* magazine listed Blair as an example of what the writer called "letterhead hires" and "invisible men." Such hires, the author continued, "enjoy a fairly carefree existence":

> Often, they're sent around the world as emissaries for their employer, tasked with giving speeches and schmoozing clients, and occasionally asked to pull out their Rolodexes to nudge a well-placed contact on some deal or regulatory issue. The job title given to a letterhead hire is often "senior adviser," and while the post can be more involved than being a board member, it's less taxing than being a day-to-day manager. Letterhead hires typically have no direct reports, no live deals, and rarely interact with the rank and file. (I once told a junior JPMorgan Chase banker that I'd seen his "co-worker" Tony Blair, the former British PM turned JPMorgan adviser, on TV. His response—"Tony Blair works here?!"—tells most of the story.)

Blair is also an envoy for the "quartet," the Middle East peacemaking group consisting of the US, Russia, the United Nations, and the European Union, and he's established three nonprofit smiley face initiatives: the Faith Foundation, which "aims to promote respect and understanding about the world's major religions"; Breaking the Climate Deadlock, which works to "bring consensus on a new and comprehensive international climate policy framework"; and the African Governance Initiative, which is "underpinned by the principle … that effective governance and political leadership are essential for delivering the public services and nurturing the thriving private sector that will create sustainable development," according to those groups' Web sites.

No one knows for sure just how much money Blair has made, but the *Financial Times* estimated that in 2011 alone he raked in at least $30 million in speaking fees and for advising governments and corporations. He and his wife own seven homes, including a £40 million (approximately $64 million), seven-bedroom property once owned by Sir John Gielgud. Blair's transformation into a human cash register has outraged many in Britain, and all the more so as he continues to collect a pension and allowance for a private office that costs taxpayers more than £122,000 (approximately $200,000) per year. Blair's "love of money" has brought about his complete "moral decline and fall," Nick Cohen wrote in a column in the *Observer*.

Blair isn't the first prime minister to cash in after leaving Downing Street. His predecessor John Major took a senior position with the American private equity firm Carlyle Group, and Margaret Thatcher netted $500,000 (about £305,000) in consulting fees from Philip Morris. But they were far more discreet and restrained than Blair in their business dealings, and both seemed more interested in political and private pursuits than in getting rich. Major in particular kept a low profile and dedicated much of his time to his greatest passion, cricket, even joining the executive committee of the organization that makes and reviews the rules of the game.

But Blair hasn't gotten heat just because he discovered that getting rich is glorious. Major and Thatcher were Tories and advocates of untrammeled capitalism, so their commercial activities didn't carry any whiff of hypocrisy. Blair moved the Labour Party to the right, but he criticized Conservative Party free-market excesses, writing (in 1996, the year before he became prime minister) that Tory promises of an "economic miracle in which income and wealth would trickle down from the top and benefit the rest of us" had instead left "a growing number of people at the bottom without work and often without hope."

Blair's friend and political doppelgänger Bill Clinton (estimated net worth: $38 million) is also making huge sums of money from speechifying and consulting, and he and his foundation have also taken money from an assortment of dubious sources. But even Clinton has been slightly more discerning in picking clients. He made introductions in Kazakhstan for Canadian mining magnate Frank Giustra; Blair, as we'll see, went directly on the Kazakh regime's payroll.

Rachel Grant, a spokeswoman for Blair's office, defended his pecuniary activities in an e-mail she sent me:

> There is nothing "inappropriate" about how Mr. Blair makes his money. Paid speeches are a completely routine way of former leaders earning money, and the speeches are mainly done through the Washington Speakers Bureau. He will also regularly donate the proceeds to charity ... As for consultancy, again this is done by many former people in senior positions, and all the work carried out is done in accordance with best business practice.
>
> The businesses help support the charity side. In the past few years Mr. Blair has given significant amounts of his income to the charities, in addition to the whole of the proceeds of his autobiography ... He spends approximately two thirds of his time on pro bono work—charity and of course his role as Quartet Representative.

Yet it's not always clear which hat Blair is wearing while traveling the globe, or if he's leveraging his allegedly humanitarian ventures to grease the wheels of his business activities. Consider, for example, his dealings with Muammar Gaddafi. Blair formed a personal friendship and geopolitical alliance with the colonel during his years as prime minister and held six private meetings with the colonel after leaving Downing Street.[3] "He kept in touch with Colonel Gaddafi after he left office and visited a number of times," Rachel Grant told me. "But he also constantly urged reform of Libya's system and to get it to open up.[4] His last visit was in 2009, and he had not visited in the two years before the uprising. He has never made money from Libya, and when Gaddafi attacked his own people last year, Mr. Blair made it clear he fully supported the action to protect the Libyan people against those attacks."

But what exactly were his meetings with Gaddafi about, and on whose behalf and dime did they take place? Grant told me rather vaguely that the meetings were "primarily on the subject of Africa," so maybe he went to Tripoli for the African Governance Initiative? Or, since he wrote a note to Gaddafi on Quartet letterhead after one meeting, perhaps he went to discuss Middle East peace? Or, as sources told the *Telegraph*, maybe he was there "sounding out deals for JPMorgan"? Yet another possibility is that he was scoping out deals for Tony Blair Associates, since after one 2008 meeting he wrote Gaddafi to thank him for his "hospitality during my visit to Libya and for taking the time to meet with me" and to emphasize that he was "particularly interested in what you said about the funds that will be dedicated to projects in Africa, since you know I am doing a lot of work there and know of good, worthwhile projects for investments."

Or maybe Blair met with Gaddafi for all those reasons? It's impossible to know.

For a man who made quite a fuss calling for transparency while in government (i.e., promoting the Extractive Industries Transparency Initiative), Blair is remarkably nontransparent about his personal moneymaking. He discloses little about his clients, contracts, or income, and TBA itself has no Web site and is entirely unmentioned on the Web site for the office of Tony Blair.

Blair has set up a complex, deliberately opaque corporate structure that makes it impossible to know how much money he's making or precisely where it's coming from. His lawyers and accountants established eight separate corporate entities to handle his business affairs, two of which are limited partnerships that don't have to publish their accounts. "What has our former prime minister got to hide?" asks Richard Murphy, an accountant and founder of the London-based Tax Justice Network. "Whatever it is, he's willing to spend good money to keep it hidden." Blair has thus far declined to accept a peerage that he is entitled to as a former prime minister, which Murphy suspects owes to the fact that he'd have to disclose his income to the House of Lords if he does so.[5]

Whatever one thinks of his politics, Blair as prime minister delivered some memorable speeches. However, the huge sums that he currently commands are something of a mystery. In style and delivery he is so boring as to make a stuffed shirt like Mitt Romney sound like Malcolm X, and the content of his private sector lectures are stunningly banal and pedestrian. "When things are in the balance, when you cannot be sure, when others are uncertain or hesitate, when the very point is that the outcome is in doubt; that is when a leader steps forward," he observed in a 2008 speech in Beijing. At a conference on Africa last year he said that there was "something wonderful, vibrant and exciting" about the continent's culture and traditions, and, speaking of economic development, helpfully pointed out, "With electricity, given the technology we now have at our fingertips, everything is possible. Without it, progress will be depressingly slow. Likewise with roads and often ports."

From scanning public accounts it appears that Blair's most lucrative speaking gigs came in March 2009, when he traveled to the Philippines and raked in more than $600,000 for two short speeches. He thereby pocketed over the space of about sixty minutes what it took him two years to gross as prime minister.

Blair gave the speeches during a thirty-six-hour visit to the Philippines, where he traveled by private jet and where he also may have achieved the apex of his oratorical banality. The first talk, called "The Leader as Nation Builder in a Time of Globalisation," was sponsored by a telecommunications company and held at a luxury hotel in Manila. "Politics really matters, but a lot of what goes on is not great," Blair told the audience. Other insights: "Politicians are a very strange people"; religion can be "a source of inspiration or an excuse for evil"; and "helping people is a noble profession, but not noble to pursue."

A second talk, held at Ateneo de Manila University, was titled "The Leader as Principled Negotiator." One account by a person in attendance quoted scintillating observations on religion ("The most important thing is to get people together"); globalization ("The most important thing is ... [to] have a driving commitment to justice"); Obama (the main problems he faces "are essentially global in nature"); and education ("In my view, [it] is what will make the difference in the future").

Another memorable speech of Blair's was delivered in 2007 in China, for which he netted £200,000 from the

Guangdong Guangda Group, a local real estate company. Blair spoke to a group of businessmen, government officials, and clients of his host at a "VIP banquet" in the industrial city of Dongguan. During his speech, titled "From Greatness to Brilliance," he said, "The reason I am in Dongguan now is because I was told that everything that was happening here was amazing. If you keep a forward-looking attitude and keep an eye on what lies ahead, Dongguan's future is immeasurable." As Blair likes to do in his speeches, he made sure to insert a reference to his personal "connection" to the country where he was speaking. In this case he did so by noting that his young son, Leo, was studying Mandarin at school.

Blair's twaddle infuriated Chinese newspapers, which said his empty remarks showed he was only interested in "digging for gold" and "money-sucking." A writer in *China Youth Daily* skewered Blair, writing:

> Frankly, we are very familiar with all this—it's just like listening to any county or city official's reports. Why pay such a high price to hear the same thing? Is it worth the money? Do these thoughts multiply in value because they come from the mouth of a retired prime minister?

Blair's consulting work has also been quite lucrative and has required the same limited exertions as his speaking gigs. The first deal that Blair closed after leaving Downing Street, according to disclosure records he filed with the Advisory Committee on Business Appointments, was inked in late 2007 with JPMorgan Chase, which reportedly pays him

$3 million annually. The firm appointed Blair as an adviser to CEO Jamie Dimon and to the company's senior management team. Blair would be "drawing on his immense international experience to provide the firm with strategic advice and insight on global political issues and emerging trends," said a press release issued by the company at the time. The statement said Blair would also "participate in select events and conferences for the company, including senior-level client events, and will provide briefings on political trends to the firm's Board of Directors."

Little is known about Blair's work at JPMorgan. The *Telegraph* newspaper has reported that he used his post at the Quartet to promote two contracts in Palestine with British Gas and mobile phone firm Wataniya, both of which are JPMorgan clients.

Much of Blair's known consulting work has been for energy-rich governments or oil companies. For example, the government of Kuwait reportedly paid his firm £1 million to advise it on governance in December 2007 and £27 million (about $44 million) on a second contract signed three years later to conduct a broad review of the Kuwaiti economy.

One suspects that the huge fees are due in large part to the gratitude Kuwait's royal family feels for Blair, due to his support for the overthrow of its archenemy, Saddam Hussein. Blair has also forged a close relationship with the emir of Kuwait, Sheikh Al-Sabah, who made an official visit to Britain (and met the queen) shortly before Blair left office.

Blair traveled to Kuwait for the Quartet in September 2007, just ten weeks after stepping down as prime minister, and the royal family held a banquet in his honor. He was back in Kuwait on another Quartet mission that December. One can surmise that he was also negotiating personal business while there, because, also in December, he reported to ACOBA that the Kuwaitis had offered him a job as an adviser on governance. He took up the post the following July, though it was more than another year before the committee disclosed the contract. Blair says he kept the deal secret at the insistence of the Kuwaitis.

Blair was again in Kuwait on Quartet business in January 2009 and was accompanied by his former aide Jonathan Powell. That's curious, because Powell didn't work for the Quartet, though the following month he was put on the payroll at TBA as a senior adviser.

At some point between then and December 2010 (when accounts appeared in the press), Kuwait gave TBA its huge contract to conduct a review of its economy and to produce a report, "Kuwait Vision 2035," examining the kingdom's political and economic future. Blair has denied the media accounts saying his firm received £27 million; he says the contract was for quite a bit less than that, though he won't be more specific. And because the deal was handled by the emir's personal office, it was exempt from any oversight by Kuwaiti agencies.

When asked by Channel 4 why Blair's firm got the deal, a former finance minister replied forthrightly, "He's very popular. For us he was a great guy to support the overthrow of the Saddam Hussein regime."[6] Nasser Al Abolly, a Kuwaiti prodemocracy advocate, told the network that the price for Blair's work was "exorbitant" and that his report was unoriginal and made recommendations similar to those in previously commissioned (and cheaper) studies.

In August 2008, according to British news accounts, Blair was retained (for an unknown fee) to advise a consortium of investors led by the UI Energy Corporation, a South Korean oil firm with major interests in Iraq. He convinced ACOBA to keep the deal hidden for nearly two years due to "market sensitivities." Blair claims that his advice is unrelated to business in Iraq and that the South Korean firm had demanded the secrecy. The deal was finally disclosed when ACOBA grew weary of Blair's continued requests to keep it hidden. Members of Parliament were not pleased when they learned of the deal in 2010. "This doesn't just look bad, it stinks," Tory Douglas Carswell told the *Daily Mail*. "It seems that the former prime minister of the United Kingdom has been in the pay of a very big foreign oil corporation and we have been kept in the dark about it. Even now we do not know what he was paid or what the company got out of it."

Liberal Democrat Norman Baker added: "These revelations show that our former prime minister is for sale—he is driven by making as much money as possible. I think many people will find it deeply insensitive that he is apparently cashing in on his contacts from the Iraq war to make money for himself."

He's certainly cashed in handsomely in the Caspian, including in Kazakhstan, which has reportedly paid his firm at least $25 million since 2011. Blair, incidentally, developed a friendship and close working relationship with President Nazarbayev while serving as prime minister. When the

Kazakh leader came to London on a state visit in 2001, he was famously photographed holding baby Leo in his arms as a beaming Tony looked on proudly.

A Kazakh source familiar with Blair's local endeavors said that as part of his deal, the former prime minister is expected to help buff Nazarbayev's "personal image ... in the international arena." And Blair has buffed away. He has publicly spoken of the Kazakh leader's political "reform program" and appeared in a dreary neo-Stalinist–style propaganda video called In the Stirrups of Time, which was produced by a Kazakh satellite channel and released in 2012. It featured extensive interviews with Nazarbayev and Western energy executives praising him, as well as fawning interventions from Blair, who says that the Kazakh dictator had displayed "the toughness necessary to take the decisions to put the country on the right path." At another point he chimes in, "In the work that I do there I've found them really smart people, capable, determined, and proud of their country."

Rachel Grant would not comment on Blair's fee in Kazakhstan, but she said he was "well aware of the criticisms made of the Kazakhstan government but would point out that there are also visible signs of progress in Kazakhstan that mark it out in the region: Over the past twenty years, GDP reached double-digit growth with impressive impact on social indicators; it has renounced its nuclear weapons, something President Obama praised in his press conference recently with President Nazarbayev; it is a majority-Muslim country of religious tolerance and one of the few to have built a synagogue in recent years;

and it has played a key role in supporting the allied effort in Afghanistan."

This justification seems entirely self-serving and elides key facts. Kazakhstan's GDP has grown, but that's been entirely on the basis of its huge energy reserves. Corruption is still rife, and governance issues have worsened, not improved. And while it's nice that Nazarbayev renounced nuclear weapons (back in 1991, not a new development) and built a synagogue, these issues have nothing to do with demonstrating his government's commitment to "reform."

Indeed, on the topic of the government's "reforms," it's not clear what Blair or his office is referring to. In June 2012 Human Rights Watch issued a report that detailed "significant setbacks" in Kazakhstan's record, including the use of criminal charges for "inciting social discord" (which carries a maximum sentence of twelve years in prison) against a number of civil society activists. The report also highlighted police and military violence against striking oil workers and their supporters in December 2012—several months after Blair began working in support of Nazarbayev's alleged reforms—when twelve unarmed protesters were shot dead.

Furthermore, even if Blair is indeed promoting reform, he's also helping market the Kazakh regime. As part of his deal, Blair's office put together a team of international advisers and consultants "to boost the reform program." Exactly who is on this team is unknown, but it includes personnel from Portland, a London PR shop that signed up to work for Nazarbayev last year, and whose senior officials include several of Blair's former top aides.[7]

Blair has also done well for himself in Azerbaijan, though in that case it was a one-off speaking event in 2011 that netted him about one hundred thousand pounds from Nizami Piriyev, one of the wealthiest men in the country and the owner of a methanol manufacturing company called AzMeCo. Piriyev has extensive holdings and political contacts across Central Asia and in Russia and the Middle East.

While in Azerbaijan Blair expressed upbeat views about President Aliyev, describing him as a leader with a "very positive and exciting vision for the future of the country." During his speech he shilled for Piriyev's newly opened methanol plant with a mix of green platitudes about "sustainable" and "responsible" growth and shameless name-dropping: "I had this conversation with Al Gore about the environment, where Al says to me, 'When there is a will, there is way.' But I always say to him: 'It is easier to have a will if you show that there is a way.' So this AzMeCo plant shows that there is a way!"

Blair clearly knew little about the topic he was speaking on and seemed to be mouthing lines fed to him by his local handlers. "I'm not a technical expert," he said. "I have got my lesson earlier, and as I understand, the first phase will be natural gas to methanol, then the second phase will be purge gas, which produces a by-product that will then be turned to urea and ammonia. And then the phase three will be the methanol derivatives. Have I been a good pupil?"

He even found time to praise formaldehyde, a by-product of methanol's industrial process (and a human carcinogen). He marveled: "To be honest, until I looked at the list of what formaldehyde does, I had no idea of how many parts of my life was governed by the existence of this thing. When I go back home, I will tell to my nine-year-old boy: "Stop all other studies and concentrate on formaldehyde and you will be fine!"

Azeri oppositionists were disgusted by Blair's appearance, especially his failure to note (or even allude to) the regime's record of human rights violations and political repression. During a trip to the Azeri capital of Baku in July, I met Hikmet Hajizadeh, who runs a prodemocracy think tank. In 2010, his son Adnan was sitting in a restaurant with friends when thugs burst in and viciously beat him, yet it was he who was charged with "hooliganism" and spent more than a year in jail.

The entire affair was a regime put-up job. Adnan's real crime had been to produce (along with a friend, Emin Milli, who was jailed on the same charges) a satirical video that made fun of the regime, for importing donkeys from Germany at about twenty thousand dollars a head, and suggested that either the deal was corrupt or the officials involved were no smarter than the mules they bought. "In terms of political freedom, it's like Brezhnev's Soviet Union here, but the government wants to impress Western investors," Hajizadeh told me. "That's why Blair was brought in. His speech was just for PR."[8]

Blair's work for Caspian dictators is hard to square with his rhetoric as prime minister. Back then he was an ardent champion of protecting democracy and human rights, which he cited in urging British military action against Slobodan Milosevic and in joining America's wars in Afghanistan and

Iraq. In a speech a few weeks after 9/11 he said there could be "no more excuses" for dictatorship and corruption, and called on Britain to "follow the principles that have served us so well at home—that power, wealth, and opportunity must be in the hands of the many, not the few."

Former prime minister Akezhan Kazhegeldin, whom Nazarbayev forced into exile in 1997, is dismissive of Blair's alleged effort to bring democracy to the country. "He can offer all the advice he wants, but you can't have better governance in Kazakhstan without changing the government," he told me, during an interview in London.

Mike Harris, a Labour Party critic of Blair, said this of the former prime minister: "Previous prime ministers have made money on the international speaking circuit and from their memoirs, but to go and take a large contract from the autocratic leader of a foreign state as an adviser is a different matter entirely ... He's deluded if he thinks that dictatorships will open up and develop into democracies through his counsel."

So what drives the former prime minister? "Blair is transfixed by money," Peter Oborne, chief political commentator for the *Daily Telegraph*, told me. "This sort of behavior is more common in America, where the culture is more commercial and presidents—in particular Bill Clinton—have acted in a financially unscrupulous fashion after leaving office. But for a British prime minister, Blair's profiteering is unprecedented in scale and shamelessness."

For Oborne, Blair's dodgy corporate setup, combined with his "long and proven track record of making false statements in matters great and small" (most famously but not limited to his allegations in regard to Saddam Hussein's alleged stockpiles of WMDs), make it impossible to take him at his word about his current earnings. "He has a history of being economical with the truth, so anything he says about his personal finances is not entirely credible. It might be true and it might not."

John Kampfner, a former editor of the *New Statesman*, believes that Blair is motivated by fame as much as cash. "Blair loved being on the world stage, and then he was forced out of office against his will," told me. "His business deals allow him to remain on the stage and continue to hobnob with the rich and powerful."

Tony Blair has not gone so far (at least yet) as to promote the Uzbek regime of Islam Karimov, a Soviet-era hack in power since 1991. But while Uzbekistan does not have official lobbying representation in Washington, it has many American friends advocating on its behalf—and because they don't register as lobbyists, it's hard to know exactly what they're up to. Chief among them is the American-Uzbekistan Chamber of Commerce (AUCC), whose board is made up of executives from US companies with interests in Uzbekistan, such as Boeing, Honeywell, and General Electric. The group's stated purpose, as described on its Web site, is to "promote trade and investment," but it also pushes for "strong ties" between the two governments on the basis of its "excellent working relations" with both.

The AUCC is chaired by attorney Carolyn Lamm, a former head of the American Bar Association who in the past has lobbied for such authoritarian states as Libya and the former Zaire, when it was ruled by strongman Mobutu Sese Seko. Between 1997 and 2005 her law firm, White & Case, lobbied for the Karimov regime. Lamm has also served as legal counsel of Zeromax, a Swiss-registered holding company widely reported as controlled by Gulnara Karimova, the president's powerful daughter. (The one described in the WikiLeaks cable as "the single most hated person in the country.")

Following the 2005 Andijan massacre—in which Uzbek security forces slaughtered hundreds of unarmed protesters —the AUCC's then president, James Cornell, wrote to then secretary of state Condoleezza Rice urging her to "not rush to conclusion or ignore the thorough investigation carried out by the government of Uzbekistan," and said that down-grading relations with Karimov threatened "several vital interests of the United States."

In 2011, AUCC board members and the Uzbek ambas-sador to Washington held a briefing with House Foreign Affairs Committee staffers. During their meeting they talked up "job creation" linked to American exports to Uzbekistan and "offered their help, expertise, and knowl-edge" for future congressional visits there. In September of the same year the AUCC held its annual business forum in Washington, which was attended by representatives of "international financial organizations, think tanks, and policy institutions" and featured speeches by Uzbek and US government officials. AUCC president Tim McGraw of NUKEM—the aptly named company that serves as an intermediary between uranium producers and nuclear energy utilities—told the crowd that his group's efforts sought to "fundamentally strengthen the overall bilateral relationship."

The same day, in what was surely no coincidence, President Obama spoke with Karimov by phone and "pledged to continue working to build broad cooperation between our two countries." This was just four days after a Senate committee, at Obama's request, voted to waive Bush-era restrictions on military aid to the Karimov dictatorship in exchange for its help moving military supplies into Afghanistan.

My request for an interview with Lamm, made through the AUCC, was declined. Elena Son, the organization's executive director, told me, "The AUCC asked the US government about the waiver for informational and better awareness purposes." The chamber, she said, was "not a lobbying organization" and its "advocacy efforts aim to inform the American public and governing institutions about why better bilateral relations with the Republic of Uzbekistan matter to US geopolitical and business interests."

Among the speakers at AUCC's business forum was Professor S. Frederick Starr of the Central Asia-Caucasus Institute (CACI) at Johns Hopkins University, who has been a reliable champion of Karimov and other former Eastern bloc tyrants. Following the 2005 Andijan massacre, Starr went on NPR and echoed Karimov's justification of the crackdown as necessary because Islamic militants were behind the demonstration. CACI later cosponsored an event (along with the Hudson Institute) that debuted a short video offering the Karimov regime's take on the

Andijan crackdown. An account of the event at EurasiaNet. org said that Starr "sought to undermine" critical reports about Andijan by saying journalists "had an anti-government agenda" and "were lying."

CACI does not disclose its donors, but over the years, an Institute brochure I obtained shows, they have included a number of US oil companies active in the region as well as Newmont Mining, which at one time had big interests in Uzbekistan; and the Joint Chiefs of Staff and the Defense Intelligence Agency. Caspian governments have funded individual scholars at CACI, which also boasted in the brochure about the Institute of its "close contacts with the Washington embassies of the various countries in the region."

In his approving comments about Caspian governments, Starr—an adviser on Soviet affairs to presidents Ronald Reagan and George H. W. Bush—sounds like one part old-line Soviet apparatchik and one part Borat. One former student of Starr's told me that he became notorious in the classroom "for his predictable whitewashing of each and every central Asian despot"—even Saparmurat Niyazov—the former leader of Turkmenistan who built a cult of personality to rival Stalin's, and who named himself "Turkmenbashi the Great." So ardent was Starr in talking up Niyazov that students took to calling him "Starrmenbashi."

Starr has been just as big a fan of Turkmenistan's new leader, Gurbanguly Berdimuhamedov, who won office in 2007 with 89 percent of the vote in an election following his predecessor's death. "I am in complete amazement from everything I have seen here!" the State News Agency of

Turkmenistan quoted Starr as saying while touring the country in November 2010.

In 2011, Starr gave a talk at CACI in which he lauded Berdimuhamedov's commitment to openness and technology. This was less than two months after Turkmenistan had shut down the country's largest mobile network. Starr also praised Berdimuhamedov's books—which include a two-volume opus on medicinal plants—which he said had allowed him to "understand the logic of the current unprecedented successes of the Turkmen government."

In a reply to a request for comment, Starr said that the purpose of his trip to Turkmenistan

> was to conduct research on a book on the eighth to the eleventh century, to visit archaeological sites connected with that work and to consult with several scholars who have conducted research on the period in question. My trip was paid for by CACI, which receives no money from Turkmenistan or any firm working there, and by me personally.

Starr has also sallied forth on behalf of Kazakhstan's President Nazarbayev. In 2008, CACI published three upbeat reports on economic and political developments in the country without mentioning that the Kazakh government had paid for them through one of its Washington lobbying firms, APCO Worldwide. Starr has even helped whitewash Kazakhstan's bogus 2004 parliamentary and 2005 presidential ballotings, as an "election observer" sent by the International Tax and Investment Center (ITIC), which is headquartered in Washington and has offices in Kazakhstan.

The ITIC is headed by Daniel Witt, a former vice president of Citizens for a Sound Economy, the predecessor organization to Dick Armey's conservative pro-business group FreedomWorks, which helped spur the Tea Party. Though it claims to be an "independent" research center, ITIC's sponsors include numerous oil companies with stakes in Kazakhstan, as well as the Kazakhstan Petroleum Association. The group's Web site even carries an endorsement from Nazarbayev. "ITIC has always insisted upon complete academic freedom for our observers," Witt told *Transitions Online Newsletter*, which reported on the organization's observer role.

While independent observers have ridiculed Kazakhstan's periodic elections, Witt and ITIC's expert teams invariably find them to be expressions of the popular will. For example, in 2004, one of the trips on which Starr served as an observer, Witt noted "vigorous and competitive activities by political parties" in what he called the "most open and competitive vote in the history of independent Kazakhstan."

Bilateral business groups like the AUCC have become an especially favored means for foreign governments and American oil companies to gain favor in Washington. For example, the departed Libyan leader Muammar Gaddafi, who Ronald Reagan once described as "the mad dog of the Middle East," came in from the cold under President George W. Bush and counted on support from the Washington-based US-Libya Business Association (USLB). That group was founded and financed by US oil companies that were unhappy about the pace at which the Washington–Tripoli relationship was developing after Bush's administration forged a rapprochement with Gaddafi's regime in 2004. Despite the political thaw there remained strong opposition in Congress to Gaddafi's regime due to his past support of terrorism. Meanwhile, European governments had been far less squeamish about embracing the colonel, giving their oil companies a leg up on American firms in the race to win concessions in Libya.

To supplement their stable of K Street lobbyists dedicated to improving ties with Tripoli, Occidental, ConocoPhillips, ExxonMobil, Marathon Oil, Chevron, and other companies set up the USLBA. According to its federal tax filings, the association sought to "educate the public on the importance of US–Libya trade and investment, and facilitate the commercial and diplomatic dialogue between the two countries." At least seven of its eight directors were registered lobbyists for oil companies.

David Goldwyn—who had served at the Energy Department under Bill Clinton, and who then ran a consulting firm that provided "political and business intelligence" to oil companies—was hired to head the group. The USLBA spent over $1 million between 2006 and 2009, of which more than six hundred thousand dollars was used to pay Goldwyn's firm. In February 2007, the USLBA brought together government officials from both countries at a gala dinner, held at the Charlie Palmer steakhouse, to honor a senior official of "The Great Socialist People's Libyan Arab Jamahiriya."

The following year, Gaddafi demanded that American

oil companies help Libya win an exemption from a law signed by President Bush that allowed American victims of terrorism to seize assets of countries found liable for attacks. Libya was a specific target of the law. The USLBA was happy to help out. Working in close collaboration with official lobbyists for Libya and the oil companies, the association urged Secretary of State Condoleezza Rice to pursue a waiver for Libya, as first reported by Bloomberg. Rice and three other Bush cabinet members soon wrote congressional leaders saying that the exemption was needed or there would be "a chilling effect on potentially billions of dollars in investments by US companies in Libya's oil sector."

Congress soon passed a measure that gave Libya the immunity it sought. Goldwyn, meanwhile, took a business delegation to Libya in December 2008 and talked about the "fantastically warm reception" they received from senior government officials.[9]

Goldwyn also served as director of the US-Turkmenistan Business Council, which was also primarily funded by American oil companies (Chevron, ExxonMobil, Marathon) hoping to do business in the country. The staff included Diana Sedney, a Chevron lobbyist. The USTBC's program included "briefings with staff members from relevant House and Senate offices"; "lunches and dinners in honor of visiting dignitaries from Turkmenistan"; and to generally "educate the public about progressive changes in Turkmenistan."

But did any "progressive" changes take place in the country under the inspired leadership of its new ruling dentist? Very little, based on news reports and independent observers. "Politically motivated harassment, detentions and imprisonments continue unabated in Turkmenistan despite the government's promises to uphold human rights," Amnesty International reported in 2011. Turkmenistan remains "one of the most repressive and authoritarian states in the world," Human Rights Watch said the same year. "Its policies and practices are anathema to European values."

The Turkmen Initiative for Human Rights, which is headed by Farid Tukhbatullin, a former political prisoner who now lives in Vienna, has also detailed regime abuses. "The new president talked about reforms, but it's been mostly cosmetic," he said. "All the schools feature his portraits and quotations from his speeches are prominently displayed. The education system is still mostly about ideological indoctrination."

Berdimuhamedov's ascension to power has been an "emotional blow" to the exiled opposition, Tukhbatullin said. "Niyazov was very old and there was hope we could outlive him," he said. "The new president is relatively young; he may outlive us."

Goldwyn joined the Obama administration in 2009 as the State Department's coordinator for international energy affairs. He resigned two years later and returned to the private sector as an energy consultant. Goldwyn declined a request for comment about his work for Libya other than to say, in response to a question about why he had never registered as a lobbyist for the USLBA, that he was not legally required to because he didn't spend sufficient hours to trigger the disclosure rule.

6

The Lobbyists: Louisiana

Who took on the Standard Oil men
And whipped their ass
Just like he promised he'd do?
Ain't no Standard Oil men gonna run this state,
Gonna be run by little folks like me and you.

—"Kingfish," Randy Newman

You talk about the junk you do like you talk about climbing trees.
You live the life of a little kid with bruises on your knees.
You will never cop to the damage that's been done.
But you will never stop 'cause it's too much fun.

—"Buttercup," Lucinda Williams

On a Monday evening in March 2013, I had a surprising, remarkably forthright two-hour conversation with Ginger Sawyer, one of the most powerful oil and gas lobbyists in the state of Louisiana. I'd called Sawyer a few weeks earlier to set up an interview and now, at about 6:00 P.M., we were sitting at a table at TJ Ribs, a restaurant in a shopping mall just off Interstate-10 in Baton Rouge, the state capital. As the wait staff carried platters of chicken fried ribs, ballpark nachos, brisket quesadillas, and other TJ specialties to surrounding tables, Sawyer and I had drinks—beer for me and red wine for her—and talked about the industry's goals and priorities for the year's state legislative session.

Louisiana is the country's the third largest energy-producing state—and first when production from its section of federally administered offshore sites is included—and far and away the biggest per capita. Since oil was discovered here in 1901, the industry has usually gotten whatever it wants. As a result, energy companies have made enormous profits while fending off any meaningful regulation. State citizens haven't done as well. Louisiana ranks near the very bottom of the states in terms of people living below the poverty line, life expectancy, and infant mortality.

Louisiana has outsized influence in shaping the national debate about energy policy. Back in the 1980s, its political and business leaders played key roles in successfully pressing the EPA to classify oil field waste as "non-hazardous" under federal rules for disposal and cleanup, decisions that saved the industry vast billions and that were made purely on political grounds, not on scientific ones. In the aftermath of Hurricane Katrina, state and federal politicians furiously demanded an early end to the Obama administration's moratorium on offshore drilling.

More recently, Louisiana's congressional delegation, led by Republican Senator David Vitter and Democratic Senator Mary Landrieu, led hysterical attacks on the EPA, including its proposed regulation, which has been bogged down in the federal bureaucracy for years, that would "add less than a penny a gallon to the cost of gasoline while delivering an environmental benefit akin to taking 33 million cars off the road," in the words of the *Washington Post*. The Louisiana lobby is also hard at work trying to ensure that final EPA environmental rules on shale fracking, which at this writing are expected to be released in early 2014, leave state governments, not the feds, with primary regulatory authority.

Sawyer, a redhead with watery blue gray eyes, is the longtime vice president of political action and chief energy lobbyist for the Louisiana Association of Business and Industry. When I'd spoken to her on the phone and asked her to suggest legislators to talk to, she not only had names but phone numbers and e-mail addresses as well, and when I subsequently mentioned her name to those lawmakers, it carried weight and opened doors. "Any friend of Ginger's is a friend of mine," Democratic State Senator J. P. Morrell had told me a few days earlier at a New Orleans coffee shop in the French Quarter when I thanked him for seeing me. "She's helped me a lot to develop as a legislator, and I always appreciate a lobbyist who tells me, 'We need your help on this, but you better stay away from us on that.'"

Sawyer is tough, smart, and relentless, so although she announced her retirement last year, LABI called her back into action on a one-year contract because the energy industry was facing major political challenges. Among them was a tax plan from Governor Bobby Jindal that would eliminate the state's corporate income tax and replace the lost revenue by jacking up the sales tax. Sawyer had no objection in principle to cutting corporate taxes but worried that raising the sales tax would cause great public anger. "If that happens, the legislature might close some of the exemptions for the oil and gas industry," she said. "I helped win a lot of those exemptions in the eighties and nineties, so I've got the institutional knowledge and history. That's one reason LABI wanted me back"

Louisiana already spends at least $1.79 billion per year on corporate subsidies, incentives, and tax breaks, with the natural resource industry being far and away the biggest beneficiary. For example, operators of low-producing stripper wells pay sharply reduced taxes because, Sawyer told me, they'd otherwise have to shut down. "That will be on the table this year, but I doubt the legislature will monkey with it, because they don't want to lose production from those reserves." Another exemption, which Sawyer said would be the biggest fiscal issue before the legislature, gives companies a tax holiday of two years on wells drilled horizontally. "Vertical drilling is easier, you go straight down and hopefully something comes up," she said with a laugh. "Horizontal wells are more complicated and expensive, which is why they get the break."

Sawyer, though, wasn't planning to merely protect current exemptions. She also hoped to win back an old one, which expired a few years ago, for companies that reopened shutdown wells to pump out the last few drops of production. "It was good for the state, but there was a sunset on it; it needed to be reauthorized by the legislature and it slipped through the cracks," Sawyer told me. She'd realized ahead of time that trouble lurked and contacted the Department of Natural Resources (DNR), the state agency that is supposed to regulate oil and gas companies but which has historically served as the industry's protector and handmaiden. "They told me they'd take care of it, but somebody over there missed the deadline, so we lost that one," she said with an air of regret.

I'd come to Louisiana to report on a different topic, and one that in recent years has been a major preoccupation of the local energy business: so-called legacy lawsuits, with which landowners have sued companies for historic contamination of properties they leased to explore for and produce oil and gas.

Major oil companies largely moved offshore in Louisiana by the late 1980s (other than for refinery operations) and sold their onshore interests to independent producers. They left behind thousands of sites polluted by spilled oil, chemicals, and other toxins. Substantial damage was caused by a by-product of the drilling process that the oil companies benevolently refer to as "salt water" or "brine." But as the name implies, brine, which is produced in vast quantities in fracking as well as in conventional drilling, has an extremely high salt content—as much as ten times higher than ocean water—that alone makes it a grave danger to groundwater and vegetation. It also routinely contains heavy concentrations of potential carcinogens, such as benzene and naphthalene, heavy metals, such as chromium and lead, and radioactive materials.

Beginning in the 1930s, US oil companies stored brine in unsealed open pits, some as big as football fields, even though they knew that the practice was unsafe. In 1932, V. L. Martin, a committee member of the American Petroleum Institute, told colleagues that the industry was "only kidding" itself if it imagined that brine waste was not seeping from the pits and polluting the land, water, and vegetation. He said it will be "only a question of time until the opposition to the escape of our waste will become strong enough to force us, as an economical measure, to dispose of them in such a manner as will not be objectionable."

At this very time the industry had already developed a safer method to store the waste: injecting it underground in saltwater disposal wells. The first such well came on line in Louisiana in 1933, and they soon became the primary method of waste disposal. But the industry continued to use unlined pits to store brine until Louisiana finally outlawed them in the late 1980s.[1]

The oil companies also dumped brine directly into marshlands and coastal waters. Flaccid state regulators allowed them to do so under certain circumstances, but the companies often dumped brine without bothering to seek authorization or inform the state. The industry also recklessly mishandled waste containing what it calls NORM, naturally occurring radioactive material, and what others, including the National Academy of Sciences, label as TENORM, or technologically enhanced NORM, which is waste in which radiation levels are increased or concentrated as a result of industrial processes.

For decades huge quantities of brine water was discharged in Louisiana: According to a 1989 US Minerals Management Service report, oil companies were dumping

Orinda Library
Contra Costa County Library
26 Orinda Way
Orinda, Ca. 94563
925-254-2184

Customer ID: 21901021965359

Title: Iron Hans /
ID: 31901018873432
Due: 07 Oct 2014
Circulation system messages:
Item checked out.

Title: Super nature encyclopedia : the 100 most
incredible creatures on the planet.
ID: 31901051587220
Due: 07 Oct 2014
Circulation system messages:
Item checked out.

Title: I'm too fond of my fur! /
ID: 31901054620416
Due: 07 Oct 2014
Circulation system messages:
Item checked out.

Title: Geronimo and the gold medal mystery /
ID: 31901050405069
Due: 07 Oct 2014
Circulation system messages:
Item checked out.

statewide an estimated 82 million gallons of brine daily. But unlike the damage done by spills—by oil washing ashore and blackening beaches, and killing fish and seabirds—most of the harm done by brine was belowground and invisible, and now, decades later, only apparent at all with "exhaustive scientific inquiry," as a DNR report put it.

Beginning about a decade ago, Louisiana landowners began winning huge judgments against Exxon, Chevron, Shell, and BP, as well as smaller independents, in legacy lawsuits and related cases. In one case, ExxonMobil was hit with a $112 million judgment—reduced from the $1 billion originally awarded by a jury—for polluting a thirty-three-acre site near New Orleans. A Louisiana appeals court called the company's behavior "calculated, despicable and reprehensible," and said it had acted "with a callous indifference toward plaintiffs and their properties." The verdict was particularly awkward for Exxon because a state judge, Joseph Grefer, owned the property it had polluted.[2]

In addition to being costly, the legacy cases put the industry in the same unflattering light that tobacco companies and asbestos manufacturers previously found themselves. Corporate documents obtained by trial lawyers through the discovery process—like the record of V. L. Martin's remarks—show not only that the companies knew how unsafe their storage methods were, but also that they continued to use unlined pits for half a century because it was more profitable to ignore the problem.

For example, a 1986 Texaco memo acknowledged that waste seepage from the company's unlined pits had caused serious groundwater contamination at a site called Fordoche

Field. "With the method of remediation being used we are looking at over 125 years cleanup time," the memo said.

> The fastest remediation process would be to remove the soil and eliminate the source. However, this is the most expensive procedure with an estimated cost between 5 and 10 million dollars. Other remediation techniques could be used to speed up the dilution process but this would depend on how much money we are willing to spend. Presently we are using the cheapest method of remediation.

The oil industry says that legacy lawsuits amount to extortion by trial lawyers, who have made enormous contingency fees on the cases, and that damages sought in court have been vastly inflated to force companies to settle. The companies previously shut down legacy lawsuits in Mississippi, another major Gulf Coast petrostate, by getting its legislature to pass bills that keep these cases out of court and require that they be heard by a state regulatory agency—the Oil and Gas Board—over which the industry exerts enormous leverage.

The companies have been working hard to win the same victory in Louisiana, and they appear to be headed for success. They lobby through the Louisiana Oil & Gas Association, known as LOGA and headed by Don Briggs, a legendary state oilman; the Louisiana Mid-Continent Oil & Gas Association, known as LMOGA;[3] and Sawyer's LABI. On the other side are the landowners and trial lawyers, as well as farm interests, the sugar cane industry, school boards (who own a substantial amount of land polluted by the industry), and environmentalists. The last have negligible influence in Louisiana, and the trial lawyers, who represent the closest thing Louisiana has to a liberal pressure group, have seen their influence dwindle over recent years. But the broader coalition is politically formidable, especially big landowners, who are generally Republicans and include major donors to Jindal, with whom they enjoy close personal ties as well. (For example, the governor's former executive counsel, Jimmy Faircloth, represents a number of plaintiffs in legacy litigation.) As a result, Jindal, who is carefully positioning himself for a potential 2016 presidential run, has sought to stay above the fray and broker a compromise in the legislature.

Only the unusual constellation of forces arrayed against the oil industry has kept it from winning a flat-out victory. "Fortunately for us, this is industry versus industry and Republicans versus Republicans," Gladstone Jones III, a plaintiffs' attorney who has won a number of big cases, told me. "If this was just oil and gas versus trial lawyers and environmentalists, we would have been killed by now."

At TJ Ribs, Ginger Sawyer offered a similar analysis. "Governor Jindal received a lot of support from the oil industry for his losing campaign in 2003 and for his winning campaign in 2007," she told me. "The industry had a good relationship with him, and when he was elected, the companies wanted their governor to fix the legacy lawsuit problem for them. But as the governor matured"—and here Sawyer arched an eyebrow—"his relationships with individuals on the oil side were superseded by new relationships he developed." As to the legislature, Sawyer said that her chief allies were Republicans but that she had good relationships with Democrats as well. Unfortunately, that didn't always get her the votes she needed. "Walt Leger [speaker pro tempore in the House] is a lovely man, but his daddy is a class-action lawyer," Sawyer said. "Karen Carter Peterson has influence in the Senate, but her daddy is a class-action litigator, too."

Despite these obstacles, Sawyer and the oil lobby have made substantial progress. Recent bills passed by the legislature, including one approved after a bruising battle last year, gives industry-friendly DNR a much greater role in settling legacy lawsuits, especially in setting the scope and cost of clean-up awards that the companies must pay. Now if a company is found guilty in court or accepts responsibility for polluting a landowner's property, the defendant and plaintiff draw up competing clean-up plans and submit them to the DNR. It picks between them or comes up with a plan of its own, and the court of original jurisdiction makes the final call on which plan gets implemented. The process has yet to be tested, but trial lawyers fear that the courts will largely defer to DNR's recommendations.

A team of six from LABI, LOGA, and LMOGA crafted last year's bill, Sawyer told me candidly. "LOGA ran point, and we were primary support," she told me. "Don and Gifford Briggs—that's Don's son—were with me in the trenches, along with Jason Bergeron, who is in-house for Exxon and who they brought in from Houston to deal with legacy cases. We would have preferred that the cases went straight to DNR, which is the arrangement we got in Mississippi, but we can't get that in Louisiana. And quite frankly, I didn't want the court to get final approval, because that allows for a lot of home cooking, but that was the best we could do. The key thing was that we wanted DNR to pick the 'most feasible plan'—that's the term of art we used throughout the discussion—and that's what we got."

I was pleasantly surprised but taken aback by Sawyer's openness. In Washington, too, legislation routinely originates with lobbyists, whether for ExxonMobil or, less often, the ACLU. But few Beltway lobbyists would so casually claim authorship of legislation–particularly in a conversation with a journalist they barely knew—and readily describe their own strategic role in getting it passed.

Jindal's tax reform bill, Sawyer now cheerfully continued, would take up most of the current legislative session, but oil and gas lobbyists would keep chipping away at the industry's legacy lawsuit exposure as opportunities arose. But Sawyer was deeply worried about a recent Louisiana Supreme Court decision that could require oil companies to restore land they polluted to higher standards than the legislature's bill calls for. "That would undo a lot of good we've won through legislation," Sawyer told me with anguish. "There's a legislator who is holding a bill for us in case we need one this session. We're hoping the Supreme Court will rehear that case, but if it doesn't, or if the rehearing goes the wrong way, that bill might be introduced."

"The trial lawyers have a place on this earth, because at some point we all need redress," Sawyer continued. "My son was in a terrible accident in high school, and I didn't know any trial lawyers, and had to go out and find one. But lawsuits should not be used as a weapon to punish some people by enriching others, and that's what's happening with the trial lawyers in these legacy cases. Personally, I try to avoid feeding the alligators."

Once again I found myself wondering why Sawyer was telling me all of this, as if she assumed I was entirely in the industry's corner. Then, after I'd asked for the check and we waited for the waitress to return with the credit card slip, she said, "You don't look anything like your picture. I thought you were bald."

Bald Ken Silverstein. Of course. The mystery of Sawyer's candor was immediately cleared up.

I remembered, back in 2011, when I was speaking at a conference of investigative reporters in Johannesburg and was contacted by a producer for a South African TV news program and asked to come to its studio to tape an interview. I was flattered to be picked from among so many journalists attending the conference and smugly imagined, as I rode to the studio in a limousine sent to pick me up, that the interview would focus on my writings on the global oil industry, which I had come to Johannesburg to speak about.

But after going through makeup and being delivered to the set, the producer informed me that the topic of the interview was an upcoming UN conference on climate change in Durban. This came as a shock, since I don't write about global warming and had no original insights on the topic. "Let's go through your bio," the producer said, as the show's host smiled at me from a chair on the set just a few feet away. "You're the editor in chief of *EnergyBiz Insider*, right?"

With that, the explanation for my invitation was immediately cleared up, and my ego badly deflated. The producer had done a Google search and mixed me up with another journalist of the same name. That Ken Silverstein looks nothing like me—most obviously, he's bald—but we both write about energy issues. My doppelgänger, though, is a specialist who writes for industry-friendly trade publications, and (after my conversation with Sawyer) I discovered he had just written a story about the Durban conference. When I write about oil I tend to focus on corruption and the "resource curse," and until the producer mentioned it had been entirely unaware of the impending Durban gathering.

I was too embarrassed to tell the producer that she had the wrong Ken Silverstein, and there wasn't much that could be done to fix the situation at that point anyway, so I mumbled something about my title needing clarification and bluffed my way through the interview as well as I could.[4] It was the same case of mistaken identity that led to my rendezvous with Sawyer at TJ Ribs.

But as I spent more time in Louisiana, I realized that Sawyer's casual revelations weren't merely the result of her erroneous belief that she was meeting with an industry sympathizer. Louisianans are by nature forthright, and that trait seems especially pronounced in oil industry officials. Trial lawyers usually felt at least a little defensive when I asked about how much money they made on legacy cases. Landowners felt compelled to tell me they were not enemies of the industry, and that it brought jobs and growth to the state. But industry people, as the long-time rulers of their domain who controlled, when it came to natural resources, everything between the sun and ocean floor, didn't feel defensive about anything. Running the show was their natural state of affairs, and they enjoyed privileges and status that were invisible to them. Doubt, self-reflection, and guilt were little known to them, and hence they censored themselves less than most people do, even when speaking to a journalist.

Since striking oil near the town of Jennings in 1901, the industry has transformed and defined the state. During the following century, it drilled 220,000 wells, built six hundred oil-producing fields, and constructed (with massive help from the state) eight thousand miles of access canals and pipelines, most of it running through wetlands. Look at South Louisiana with Google Earth and you'll see a coastal landscape punch-holed by drilling operations and cut to ribbons by support infrastructure.

The industry's historic operations are a major reason why Louisiana's coastal wetlands are disappearing at the rate of about twenty-five to thirty-five square miles per year, one of the fastest rates in the world.[5] The canals and pipelines eliminated the natural wetlands barrier, and sucking oil and gas out of the marshes caused the land to literally cave in and disappear. The consequences range from the disappearance of a major flyway for migratory birds to the increased vulnerability of the state to hurricanes. There's no dispute, for example, that Katrina's impact was far worse because of coastal erosion.

The energy industry has also defined Louisiana politically, socially, and culturally, especially beginning with the era of Huey Long, the "Kingfish," a Democrat who was elected governor in 1928. Long's style of populism would be unthinkable in modern-day Louisiana, or anywhere else in America. He tapped into a well of resentment against big business and its allies in the political establishment in Washington and Baton Rouge. His favorite targets were the Chase Manhattan Bank, the United Fruit Company, and above all, Standard Oil and the "invisible empire" of the Rockefellers.

Long built roads, hospitals, and schools with taxes on the industry. The political and economic elite loathed him and tried to impeach him after he proposed a five-cent-per-barrel tax on the production of refined oil to help fund his social programs.

Long fought off impeachment thanks to the huge support he enjoyed from the poor—the House referred charges to the Senate, but the process was suspended when his enemies could not muster the needed two-thirds majority—and he was elected a US senator in 1932. Two years later, during the height of the Great Depression, he created the Share Our Wealth program under the motto "Every Man a King," which proposed using revenues from taxes on the rich and corporations to implement antipoverty programs.

He was assassinated in 1935—by the son-in-law of a political enemy—but his influence lives on through the current day, and his relatives have been elected to numerous state and federal posts. His brother Earl served three terms as governor (spending part of the last one in a mental hospital, where he was committed after taking up with stripper Blaze Starr), and his son Russell, who began his political career at age four licking stamps for his father, became one of the longest-serving US senators, and was once dubbed "the fourth branch of government" by the *Wall Street Journal*.

Professor Wayne Parent explained Huey Long's legacy over a cup of coffee at Pinetta's café, just outside the campus of Louisiana State University where Parent teaches state and Southern politics. It was a beautiful sunny afternoon, and we sat at an outdoor table. Parent who had a scraggly beard and a highly relaxed manner that no doubt comes from the combination of being a native-born Louisianan with a tenured faculty job at a major university. "Are you nervous?" he asked me at one point. "You really need to relax." For me, a person who normally runs at a high level of stress, it had indeed been a particularly busy day of running between interviews, and I had more scheduled until late in the evening. Parent's good-natured, cheerful disposition only served to heighten my anxiety.

Until the Civil Rights Act of 1965, most Southern politicians were Democratic, racial populists. "Huey came from an antislavery family, and he had a lot of oil and gas money to spend on social programs, so it was rich versus poor, not white versus black," Parent explained. "He was a class populist, not a race populist, and that made us very different than the rest of the South."

So did dissimilar immigrant patterns (more southern than northern European), the high number of Catholics and the corresponding influence of the Catholic Church, and a relatively liberal, tolerant, Cajun southern Louisiana. Up until the Voting Rights Act, when the black "threat" washed away class populism, racial politics were not as virulent as elsewhere in the South. Today Louisiana is hard red politically and losing its social and cultural distinctiveness, too. "We're not so different from Mississippi now, but we were very different even twenty years ago," Parent told me.

Oil and gas money not only financed Long's social projects but also greatly contributed to the corruption that Louisiana is famous for. Politicians used it to reward friends and punish enemies, and because it didn't come from taxpayers, they could spend it however they liked. "If you wanted to build a bridge and the estimate was too high, you just built the fucking bridge," Parent said as he leisurely sipped his coffee. "The attitude was, 'I don't care what it costs and no one is monitoring spending anyway.' No one cared about corruption and there was no culture of accountability until oil prices crashed in the 1980s and we lost that money. We've been trying to replace it ever since and now every politician runs as a reformer."[6]

In addition to corruption, Louisiana has come to share other characteristics with classic Third World petrostates, including glaring social inequalities and little spending on social programs. Texas, for example, dedicated a huge amount of oil and gas money to pay for educational programs, with the result that Texas A&M and the University of Texas at Austin each have current endowments of more than $1 billion. LSU, by contrast, receives so little public support that it's fundamentally a private institution.

Today there are no more Huey Longs in Louisiana politics railing against industry and advocating for the poor. Republicans embrace oil and gas as a business interest, and Democrats, a dying breed, champion it on the grounds of job creation.

Of course, oil and gas has plenty of political power at the national level, and in many other states as well. In most places, though, it exerts its influence by hiring lobbyists to pressure elected officials and regulatory agencies. In Louisiana, the industry has cut out the middlemen and prefers to put its own people in place.

For example, Republican senator Robert Adley, the chief sponsor of the industry's 2012 legacy lawsuit legislation in the upper chamber, is a former board member of LOGA and owned and operated a company called Pelican Gas Management until he sold it that year. Representative Neil Abramson, the chief House sponsor, is a New Orleans Democrat and a lawyer who represents "oil and gas companies in legacy suits involving claims of property and groundwater contamination," according to his bio. House legislator Jim Morris, another industry champion, is an oilman who represents Oil City, Louisiana. (His wife, Kellie, is events coordinator at the town's Louisiana State Oil and Gas Museum.)

The industry has also frequently been able to get its own appointed to top positions at the state's two main environmental agencies, the DNR and the Department of Environmental Quality (DEQ). The latter is charged with enforcing federal clean air, clean water, and hazardous waste laws, which the EPA says Louisiana does a worse job of than almost any other state. A 2011 EPA inspector general report said that weak enforcement at the DEQ was driven by "a lack of resources, natural disasters, and a culture in which the state agency is expected to protect industry."

The DNR is far worse. In 1989, the *New Orleans Times-Picayune* ran an astonishing multipart investigative series[7] that chronicled industry dominance over the department and its Office of Conservation, the agency with direct authority of over oil and gas. The series reported "a lack of effective oversight that allows oil field waste disposers to violate state laws for months or years without fear of significant legal reprisals." Industry was "fiercely protective of DNR's regulatory authority over oil and gas activities," said the newspaper, and its lobbyists had "waged intense battles in the Legislature in recent years against efforts to move environmental regulation of oil field activities to DEQ."

The trial lawyers have obtained documents showing that even oil companies believed that the state underregulated them. A 1980 Shell memo acknowledged that its waste pits were violating "numerous" federal and state environmental regulations, sometimes flagrantly, primarily because "the antiquated pit systems used at these fields were not designed to protect the environment." A related problem was that

state enforcement agencies have been slack in enforcing their regulations. This slackness may have been considered beneficial by management when cost was evaluated in the past, but it has created a mood of operational indifference that has in most instances resulted in poor upkeep of facilities.

B. Jim Porter was named secretary of DNR in 1984, a critical time as the majors were moving offshore and the DNR was determining rules on closing down the unlined saltwater pits that are at the center of so many of the current legacy lawsuit cases. Industry only acceded to pit closures due to mounting public anger, political pressure from Washington, and fear of future lawsuits by landowners. The public climate toward use of earthen pits is becoming hostile due to EPA enforcement activities," B. D. Freeman, a Shell employee, wrote in an April 2, 1984, memo.

Some businesses have been operating pits without regard for protection of soil and groundwater resources. EPA has cleaned up some of these pits at high cost to taxpayers, and evidence shows these pits have definitely contaminated soil and groundwater resources ... Operators must begin to design and close pits properly or lawsuits will become a severe problem in the future.[8]

The Mid-Continent Oil and Gas Association drafted the state rules on pit closures that DNR ultimately issued in 1986. (When Porter resigned from public service two years later he became the trade group's president.) The regulations gave the oil companies a three-year grace period to shut down unsealed pits. Even so, the *Times-Picayune* found "a blatant disregard of the rules by the oil industry and nearly non-existent enforcement" by DNR. Of the estimated twenty thousand oil field waste pits in Louisiana, only sixty-six had been shut down to regulatory standards when the deadline arrived in 1989, a compliance rate of less than 1 percent.

By then, J. P. Batchelor, a retired executive of AMOCO (now BP), had become head of the DNR's Office of Conservation. In a 1984 memo—one of the documents the trial lawyers later won through discovery—written when he was at AMOCO, Batchelor had proposed that instead of shutting down its dirty old unlined pits, the company donate them to landowners for use as duck or fishponds. "Donations of drilling pits would be beneficial as we would be relieved of the obligation to backfill," Batchelor wrote. He estimated the cost to backfill a drilling pit at between $15,000 and $20,000. Of his agency's failure to force compliance with pit closure rules, Batchelor told the *Times-Picayune*:

> It would take a hell of a long time to check out each of the pits. But you know, the State Police aren't catching everyone that's speeding. They've got to depend on people to be honest and abide by the law, and that's what we do.

Between 2004 and 2012, Scott Angelle was secretary of the DNR. In 2010, he founded the Back to Work Coalition, which was comprised of twelve oil and gas industry groups and created to fight new federal regulations on the industry. In 2011 he was honored by LMOGA for his "exceptional environmental stewardship" following the Deepwater Horizon "incident," in the delicate phrasing on an association press release. He resigned from DNR soon after an underground salt production cavern run by Houston-based Texas Brine—it produces brine for the petrochemical industry—collapsed below the Bayou Corne waterway in a poor area about forty-five miles from Baton Rouge. That created a massive sinkhole 700 feet in diameter and 210 feet deep and required the evacuation of about 150 nearby residents. After leaving DNR, Angelle was elected to the Public Service Commission, the utility regulatory body where Huey Long got his start in politics.

Some trial lawyers told me that they have hopes the DNR will be less partial to industry under its new secretary, Stephen Chustz, but the department has a fundamental conflict at its core: It is supposed to regulate the oil and gas industry, but it also gets its budget funds from leasing state land for energy development and collecting royalties from production. "DNR has a conflict of mandate and mentality," says Oliver Houck, a Tulane University law professor and author of a 2006 report called "Can We Save New Orleans?"[9] "It is an appendage of the industry with zero independence." The essential context of legacy lawsuits, Houck told me, is that the oil companies devastated the environment with DNR's tacit blessing, leaving the courts as the only option for landowners to get their properties cleaned up. All of which explains why the oil industry so desperately wants to move legacy lawsuits out of the courts and put them before the DNR.

One night in Baton Rouge I had dinner with trial attorney Don Carmouche at Ruffino's—a restaurant featuring Frank Sinatra and Tony Bennett on the soundtrack, photos of the Brat Pack on the walls, and generous portions of veal parmesan and multiple crab-stuffed meat and fish options. At my request, Paul Templet, a former head of the DEQ, joined us for dinner.

Templet, who has salt-and-pepper hair and sported a big gut beneath an orange dress shirt, ran DEQ between 1988 and 1992, under Republican Governor Buddy Roemer (a little noticed candidate for the GOP presidential nomination in 2012). Roemer is the only Louisiana governor of modern times who made a serious effort to reform state government, and he picked political appointees on the basis of merit, not patronage. He was defeated after his first term by Edwin Edwards, who later was sentenced to ten years in prison on racketeering charges, whereupon Templet lost his job.[10]

A former professor of environmental studies at LSU who holds a PhD in chemical physics and a master's in physical chemistry, Templet frequently testifies for Carmouche as an expert witness. "I know that oil is valuable, but so is land and water," he said as he reached for the breadbasket. "The oil companies don't look at the long term. These lawsuits at least help get them to think about that." For Templet, environmental rules are a means of "internalizing externalities" by making polluters pay the costs of pollution, not taxpayers. "The oil companies want to externalize their costs," he said. "If they can, they'll find a cheap way to dispose of their waste, like those unlined pits, and get landowners or the public to pick up the tab."

Carmouche, who'd just turned seventy-two during a vacation in Florida with a retired judge, looked tanned and rested. He was short, with thinning hair, and he wore a black shirt, dark pants, and low-cut black boots. Carmouche is less slick than the other major trial lawyers who pursue legacy cases. He was raised in Napoleonville, a small town where he was elected and served as district attorney for six years.

For reasons I could never entirely figure out, the industry side loathes Carmouche more than the other big trial lawyers—and they dislike all of them pretty intensely—though possibly it's because he's been at it longer, twenty-five years, and started before juries and judges began making big awards in the cases. In 2001, his firm won a settlement from an energy company over a gasoline plume emanating from its processing plant that migrated to an old woman's neighboring land and polluted it so badly that neighbors used her well water to run their lawnmowers.

Carmouche shared with me some especially damning documents he'd obtained through the discovery process. There was a March 27, 1986, Unocal (now part of Chevron) memo that said that the company would be required to clean up about three hundred old polluted sites under the DNR's new regulations. Though, the memo also said, that on the positive side, Unocal's lobbyists had in the past "been effective in tempering state bills and proposed regulations which would have increased clean-up and disposal costs. Identified savings exceed some $20 million." An ARCO (now a BP subsidiary) memo from two months later noted that the company had told the state that its pit disposal practices were "adequate" to prevent seepage and pollution. "This position is actually our formal position to the public rather than the consensus of environmental professionals within ARCO," the memo's author conceded. "There are some real concerns within ARCO that pit disposal practices may be inadequate to protect the environment."

While we drank red wine and waited for the food, Carmouche explained that the trial attorneys have over the years been able to significantly expand the scope of discovery. "For years the companies argued that they should only have to turn over documents on a given oil field. We'd say, 'Judge, there are documents relating to corporate policy we'd like to see,' and after a while the judges decided that was relevant, and we'd get those. We've become more sophisticated; now we hire companies that do what's called 'predictive coding' to help search their databases. But first we have to find the documents, because a lot of companies now set up separate entities that own and store them, so we can no longer go to the company directly. When we finally get authorization to search those databases, that's when the cases settle, because it's their own documents that damn them. In some cases we never even see the documents, but we know they must have been hot or otherwise they wouldn't have settled."

Carmouche doesn't like the term "legacy lawsuits," which originated with the industry and suggests, as he sees it, that the cases have no current relevance, because they involve pollution originating decades ago. But, he said, the term is accurate in one sense: "They left a legacy of shit."

Landowners began filing legacy lawsuits decades ago, but the threat they posed did not fully capture the industry's attention until 2003, when the state supreme court upheld a $33 million judgment—far bigger than any prior award—against Shell in a case brought by a landowner named William Corbello. The ruling said Shell "exercised calculated business acumen" in using cheap, unlined pits to store salt water on the plaintiff's property because it "behoove[d] them to breach the contract in this manner and thereby reap substantial financial savings."

Even worse for industry, Corbello v. Shell established that punitive damages could exceed the fair market value of the polluted property, which meant there was essentially no cap on how much plaintiffs could win. The court ruled that limiting damage to market value "would give license to oil companies to perform its operations in any manner, with indifference as to the aftermath of its operations because of the assurance that it would not be responsible for the full cost of restoration." Furthermore, the ruling did not require landowners to use damages payments to restore their properties but could, if they chose to, pocket the settlement.

Legacy cases are extremely expensive to bring, and plaintiffs cannot be sure they will prevail in court, but there's no doubt that the big payout and terms of the Corbello case emboldened landowners and trial lawyers to try their luck in court, and sometimes with flimsy facts to support their claims. However, many cases over the years have involved vast, well-documented environmental damage to landowners' properties.

In 2007, ExxonMobil and a number of other companies were found responsible for poisoning eighteen thousand acres of coastal land owned by William Doré—who'd made a fortune in the oil services business and owned a company that belonged to LOGA—with hydrocarbons, lead, arsenic, and cadmium. Fish and crabs around the property were found to contain levels of pollutants that made them "unfit for human consumption," a court ruled. Documents introduced by the plaintiff show that in 1942 a state agency warned a predecessor firm of Exxon that brine could kill marshland and fish, but the company continued to improperly dump it on his property for the next thirty-one years. Exxon was assessed damages of $57 million to settle.

The attorney in the case was Gladstone Jones, whose twenty-fifth-floor office in the New Orleans business district offers a sweeping view of the city and a long stretch of the Mississippi River. It was the end of the workday, and Jones's pinstriped jacket was hanging in a corner, and he'd unloosened his blue-and-silver tie. "Right here in this building we called in the defendants, including Exxon, and told them we'd shut down the case if they cleaned up Bill's property," he said as he sat back in his chair and rested his feet on the desk. "They refused, and we filed the lawsuit, and after spending $4.5 million on it, we won."

Jones has made good money through contingency fees on legacy cases, for which he offers no apology. "The oil companies don't like the fact that we make a good living, and we do make a good living," he told me. "We also provide a very good service to the people of Louisiana."

Jones has been involved in about thirty legacy lawsuits overall, starting fifteen years ago. "In every one I have to file a lawsuit, and every time I do the oil companies have to file a response," he said. "Not one time has an oil company ever said, 'We operated on your property and we caused a mess and we're going to clean it up.' They've never learned the lesson taught to the rest of us by our mothers, which is you do the right thing and clean up your own mess."[11]

A more recent client of Jones's is former governor Mike Foster, a conservative Republican who while in office rammed through a sweeping "tort reform" package that severely restricted plaintiffs' ability to seek punitive damages in auto insurance claims. "Mike and I were not on the same page when he was governor," Jones said, as he shifted his feet on the desk to find a more comfortable position. "He was very aggressive in sticking up for the oil companies, so you can imagine my surprise when he called me in 2010 to report that he had a little problem with Exxon and asked would I perhaps be interested in representing him."

The little problem, which led to a lawsuit Jones filed in March 2010, involved a property Foster owned in St. Martin Parish. Oil field waste discharged by Exxon, including brine, contaminated Foster's land with oil and grease, barium, cadmium, chromium, lead, zinc, and mercury.

By 1984, Exxon knew that a bulkhead—essentially a restraining wall—surrounding a massive waste pit was eroding but failed to repair it. Three years later an Exxon engineer wrote a memo saying that repair of the bulkhead was now "an operational necessity," as it posed "a safety and pollution hazard." Yet no repairs had been made three months later when a DNR inspector flew over the facility. "Some aquatic invertebrate and fish mortality expected— fish flesh probably tainted to taste," said a report he filed.

"Three to four acres of marsh/swamp have been destroyed, probably as a result of long-term leaking problem."

Exxon ultimately settled the case on undisclosed terms; Jones now represents Foster in another case against the company on a separate piece of property. "I never thought I'd support right-wing Republicans, but as luck would have it, many of them believe in landowners' rights," he told me. "It's an odd demographic of supporters we find, but in these coastal parishes people have lived off the land for generations, hunting, fishing, and trapping. They don't care much about material things other than their property. Oil is money, land is family."

Indeed, the political geography of legacy lawsuits is surprisingly complex. The trial lawyers have alliances with Republicans politicians such as Foster and rich GOP landowners such as Roy Martin, a plaintiff in several legacy cases who, like Doré, owned an oil company and was a member of LOGA, and who is close to Jindal. In December 2012 there was a race for a seat on the state supreme court between Republican Jeff Hughes, who describes himself as "pro-life, pro-gun, and pro-traditional marriage," and John Michael Guidry, an African-American Democrat from Baton Rouge. The trial lawyers backed Hughes, who also is pro–property rights, and poured massive funding into his campaign through a super PAC they created, while energy companies supported Guidry. Hughes won a close race, which sent tremors throughout the industry.

Then there are urban Democrats like J. P. Morrell, the senator from New Orleans who spoke so fondly of Sawyer and who sides with industry on legacy lawsuits. He represents what he described as a "classic gerrymandered district," which was designed under the Voting Rights Act to ensure that African Americans are better represented in Congress and state legislatures. It starts across the street from CC's, a coffee shop at Royal and St. Philip Street in the French Quarter, where we met, and runs across the 13,428-foot Crescent City Connection bridge to the city's West Bank in one direction and into St. Bernard Parish in the other. Morrell's mother serves on the New Orleans City Council and his father was a House member in the state legislature for twenty-four years and is now the city clerk. Morrell won his father's House seat in 2006 and was elected to the Senate two years later in a special election called when his predecessor was indicted by the feds on money-laundering charges.

Morrell was wearing a blue suit with a Senate pin on his jacket lapel. He had a neatly trimmed beard and slicked-back hair, and his smartphone and tablet lay on our small table. Morrell told me that Jindal's tax plan amounted to "screwing the poor by trying to balance the budget with sales and cigarette taxes." The Sierra Club endorsed him during his last campaign, and he had "a history of being environmentally conscious."

How, I asked him, had he ended up on the oil industry's side in the legacy fight? "Conservative landowners in rural districts fund the candidates in their districts, and they are beholden to them," he replied. "Urban legislators tend to be Democrats, and they don't have large landowners in their districts, so we can look at this more logically."[12] Morrell offered an impassioned but curious defense of the industry's position: "Look, when a landowner leases his land for oil exploration, he's pretty much giving the company permission to pillage it. They profited for all those years from allowing their land to be pillaged, and then, when all the oil is sucked out of it, they say, 'I want to be paid for the damages.' Yes, the land should be cleaned up, but they're profiting on both ends, and there's a huge disparity between how much money the trial lawyers say is needed to clean up and what the oil companies say."

Morrell believed the oil company estimates were generally closer to what should be awarded.

I received an equally interesting lesson in legacy lawsuit politics when I visited with Don Briggs, who founded and lobbies for LOGA, in Baton Rouge. Briggs grew up in Florida and came to Louisiana one summer to work on a drilling rig. He stayed for college, married a tool pusher's daughter, and in 1968 opened his own oil company. Over the years he's served on the boards of several industry groups, among them the Independent Petroleum Association of America, and been appointed to the Governor's Environmental Task Force, the Oilfield Site Restoration committee, and the Senate Select Committee on Oil and Gas Permitting.

Briggs, who is age seventy-two, wore jeans, a gray jacket, and black boots. His son, Gifford—LOGA's vice president, who Briggs called "my technician"—was a good deal shorter than his father and bore little resemblance to him other than sporting the same black boots. Don Briggs was just back in town from the association's annual conference, which was held this year at L'Auberge du Lac Casino Resort in Lake Charles and featured as a keynote speaker Sherman

Joyce, president of the Washington-based American Tort Reform Association. LOGA operates from a lovely lake-front home that once belonged to former governor Jimmie Davis—known nationally at one time for singing country ballads such as "You Are My Sunshine," which he wrote—and that sits adjacent to the current governor's mansion.

Briggs was on the phone when I arrived, and his assistant, CeCe Richter, showed me around the office. We walked through a small room off the kitchen, where bottles of Crown Royale, Dewar's, Wild Turkey, Jack Daniels, and Maker's Mark sat on a countertop, then passed a window and saw workers out back who were upgrading a large deck that faces the lake. "We do a lot of entertaining here, legislative stuff," Richter explained. "That work's been going on way too long. My son's getting married in a month, so they better hurry up."

I mentioned to Briggs that I'd already spoken with Randy Haynie, a highly influential lobbyist who works for trial lawyers on legacy lawsuits (and for many major corporations, including energy companies, on other matters), and who works from an elegant office a few blocks away, in the home of former governor Earl Long. "I drive a white car and he drives a black car," he replied. "I wear a white hat and he wears a black hat, I'm a good guy and he's a bad guy." I thought he was kidding, but when I smiled he didn't smile back.

Briggs founded LOGA in 1992, after Edwin Edwards won back his seat by defeating Buddy Roemer. The DEQ had begun regulating NORM a few years earlier under Paul Templet and, Briggs recalled, the Department also had authority to issue licenses to companies that were allowed to accept radioactive waste. "A guy by the name of Richard Brackin, who worked for DEQ, he let those permits out," Briggs said. "He was a convicted felon, I think for attempted murder, and he was awaiting a pardon, and Governor Edwards later gave him one. That was my first introduction to the way politics works here."

Briggs owned a company that rattled oil field pipes— that's a cleaning process by which a reamer is run through the pipe and air is then blown through it, thereby creating a dust storm of all the material that had been caked on it, including NORM. "The DEQ had put all these restrictions on NORM because it was going to kill everyone, which was bullshit," Briggs said. "I got pissed off, which is why I started LOGA. I was just going to get it up and running and get back into business, but I stayed and became passionate."

Time plays with memory in unexpected ways, and this nightmare tale of regulatory intrusion and government bungling did not unfold precisely as Briggs remembered, as I later learned when trying to confirm it. Brackin was a convicted felon, but for "aggravated burglary," a crime he committed in 1979 at the age of twenty-six and for which he received three years' probation, according to an account in the Times-Picayune.[13] He was later hired at DEQ, and by late 1992 had become one of its top regulators of radioactive waste. His criminal record became an issue that December when he imposed an eighteen-hundred-dollar fine on an oil company owner after his inspectors found radioactive material in three wells on the owner's property.

The aggrieved oilman happened to be then state representative and future senator Robert Adley, who introduced legislation the following May banning the employment of felons at DEQ. The bill affected only one person, Richard Brackin, who by then was acting director of his department and had infuriated the entire industry by threatening to issue fines against pipe yards that mishandled radioactive materials. The secretary of DEQ, Kai Midboe, wrote Adley promising to ease off on regulations. Brackin was given a pay cut and transferred to another section inside DEQ that didn't regulate radioactive waste (and within six months the entire DEQ division regulating such waste was decimated when key personnel were forced out or fired). An appeased Adley withdrew several other bills he'd introduced that targeted DEQ regulations. In a 1994 news story about the case, Briggs said Adley had been right to target Brackin, who he said had been practicing "environmental terrorism."

Governor Edwards did pardon Brackin on the aggravated burglary conviction in 1993, based on the recommendation of the state pardon board.

In theory, LOGA represents smaller independent oil companies and LMOGA represents the multinational giants, which is something that Briggs plays up. "The difference between our guys and the big oil companies is that we're the homeboys, we have heart," he told me. But while Briggs's members are independently owned, they are not mom-and-pop operations. They include Chesapeake Energy, the country's second-largest producer of natural gas, and ConocoPhillips, which has operations in almost thirty countries and more than sixteen thousand employees.

Furthermore, the major oil companies fund LOGA—"They should, because they caused most of the problems," he told me—and Briggs seems equally passionate about defending them. "Right now BP is getting raped and pillaged by anyone who had any sort of business on the Gulf Coast and sees an opportunity to get BP money," he told me over a brief racket of construction work from the back deck. "People say that because of the oil spill they couldn't enjoy their vacation homes on the water so they want damages for that. When you hold out twenty billion dollars"—the size of the fund Obama and BP agreed on to compensate victims of the Deepwater Horizon disaster—"everyone wants part of it."

In terms of environmental damages related to legacy lawsuits, Briggs acknowledged that the industry was not entirely innocent. "The companies didn't always clean up as they should have," he said. "If Shell had cleaned up the mess in the Corbello case, we wouldn't be sitting here having this conversation, but they pissed off the landowner, and he sued them, which set off a feeding frenzy. The same thing happed with Exxon and Billy Doré. Billy's a friend of mine, and he's a great American. He just wanted his damned land cleaned up. I flew out there in a helicopter, and I walked his property, and I know exactly the kind of problems he had. He asked Exxon to clean up, and they didn't, so he got on the other side."

Richter stepped into the room and told Briggs there was a phone call he needed to take. "Where are my monkeys?"

he asked the person on the other end of the line. When he rang off a minute later he explained that he had bought three brass monkeys and was anxious to get them. "It's a set, see, hear, and speak no evil," he laughed. "I couldn't think of a better thing to put in a lobbyist's home."

It seemed like a good time to turn the conversation to politics, so I asked whether the industry had inordinate political influence in Louisiana. He denied the assertion by way of a story about a visit he'd made to Houston to discuss the political fight on legacy lawsuits with the head of an oil company. "He asked me what the hell was going on, so I showed him this picture," he said, as he pulled out a page from a PowerPoint presentation that had photographs of a number of politicians and businessman and a lot of arrows that ultimately led to Governor Jindal. He pointed to the photos one at a time and provided commentary. "Mike Foster has a number of lawsuits, and he gave Jindal his first post in politics.[14] Jimmy Faircloth used to work for Jindal, and he represents Roy Martin, who has a number of lawsuits and is a big contributor to Jindal. Buddy Caldwell is the attorney general, and he says, 'I have nothing to do with any of this,' and that's bullshit, because he supports these types of lawsuits. We told the governor we need help on this, but he won't help, because he's tied to all these guys ... The last thing in the world these rich Republican landowners want to do is to be tied to the trial lawyers, but they've hitched their wagon to them."

Briggs continued, picking up steam. "Mr. Carmouche is not very well liked, he's a tainted old dog, so when he gets a guy like Roy Martin on his side, that's pretty special. Meanwhile, they are fucking with dozens of my members, who are being crippled by these cases."

It certainly is true that some of Briggs's members have gotten a bad deal in legacy lawsuits. When they moved offshore, the major companies sold their onshore assets cheaply to independents, but in exchange made the new owners partially indemnify them for future liability stemming from environmental damage they may have caused. The independents liked the price they got and probably didn't realize how much liability they were taking on. Speed up twenty years, and they were left holding the bag along with the majors who caused the original damage. "Most of my guys had nothing to do with the pollution, but they're in the food chain, and so they get dragged in," Briggs said with irritation. "So every little guy has to lawyer up, and a few greedy trial lawyers are very happy."

Haynie had told me that landowners floated a proposal in 2012 that would have let the independents off the hook by making the old indemnification agreements null and void, but that LOGA had opposed that. "That's absolutely true," Briggs said with a big smile when I asked him about it. "The governor realized we were going to pass a bill, and he was getting a lot of heat from Senator [David] Vitter for being in bed with trial lawyers, and a guy who wants to move up in the Republican Party can't have that. So his guys came up with the indemnification clause for the independents. It sounded real good, and I would have liked to say yes, my life would have been easier, but you can't undo contractual obligations just because you feel like it. It would have been tied up in court for ten years and overturned in the end, because it's unconstitutional."[15]

Gifford Briggs had been walking in and out of the room, and when he next came back his father asked him to bring back something to show me. It was a copy of a PowerPoint presentation that Bill Griffin, a longtime petroleum engineer with AMOCO who frequently testifies as an expert witness for plaintiffs, gave in 2006 at the South Texas College of Law. The presentation—"A View from the Trenches: Legacy Liability in Louisiana"—has a lottery ticket on the cover, and one of the slides says, in a reference to the Corbello judgment, "$33 million looking pretty good. How do I locate areas where I may successfully litigate for environmental damages?" The next slide says to look in southern Louisiana, which offers "a rich environment of deep pockets" with at least one major oil company "on the hook." Furthermore, another slide says, "it's best to narrow one's search to southern Louisiana because salt domes and salt water from the coast may have polluted the land, but it will look like it's from oil and gas brine water."

Briggs also gave me a video of Griffin's presentation, which shows him making the same point about the region having a lot of naturally occurring salt. LOGA had put together a TV ad using the video. "What's an enterprising trial attorney to do?" asks a voice-over. "Drag Mother Nature into court."

Just about every oil industry representative I spoke with told me about Griffin's presentation and described it as a sales pitch to trial lawyers looking to find legacy cases to litigate. The presentation was covered extensively in the local press, migrated upward to Fox News, and offered as proof that legacy lawsuits are a scam to make trial lawyers rich.

Griffin himself says he was being facetious and show-boating, and the circumstances seem to support him. For example, Griffin was speaking at a conference primarily attended by industry defense lawyers, not plaintiffs' attorneys. He was invited to speak by the conference sponsor, Liskow & Lewis, which has, says its Web site, "established ourselves as leaders in energy law by counseling the most significant names in the oil and gas industry."

Whatever the circumstances, Briggs is no fan of lawyers, and that included the oil industry's own defense attorneys, who he says love legacy lawsuits, too, because they get to bill the companies for millions of dollars. "When you have a big snake you can get a shovel and cut its head off—that's one way to deal with the problem—or you can get a stick and poke the snake, and that's what the defense lawyers do," Briggs told me. "I once had a group of them sitting here in this office, and I told them, 'Congratulations, Don Carmouche and these other guys are kicking your asses.'"

At 11:15 A.M. on March 12, 2013, I was waiting impatiently beneath the shade of a live oak in front of the white-brick courthouse in Abbeville—"The Most Cajun Place on Earth," declared a roadside billboard in Lafayette, twenty miles back—to meet a man named Ron Miguez. Miguez worked for Warren Perrin, an attorney, and a lead plaintiff in a $300 million legacy lawsuit against Chevron, and Perrin had arranged for Miguez to take me to see the nearby eighty-acre property that the company had allegedly polluted. He was fifteen minutes late, so I called Miguez and asked a little testily what the delay was. "I'm supposed to get you at eleven," he said, without a trace of annoyance, in a thick southern Louisiana drawl. "By my watch, it's a little after ten." We'd switched to Daylight Savings Time two days earlier, and Miguez had forgotten to spring forward.

It was the perfect introduction to Miguez, a delightfully loopy character who picked me up in his pickup truck a few minutes later. (In Abbeville, population twelve thousand, you're never more than a few minutes from anywhere.) Six feet tall and white-mustachioed, he was wearing a cowboy hat, a leather jacket, and a checkered shirt.

After we'd driven off I asked him how he'd met Perrin. "I was in a trucking wreck twenty-five years ago and he took my case," he said. "I've worked for him ever since. I don't have a wife and kids, so it works out well for me."

"What do you do for him?" I asked.

"Just about everything," Miguez answered. "I'm his chauffeur, bodyguard, chef, patch the roof if it's needed, deliver subpoenas." With that he took both hands off the wheel and rifled through papers above the sun visors looking for, and finding, after nearly driving off the road, a subpoena to show me.

I told Miguez about attending a hearing that morning in the case between Chevron and nearly one hundred heirs of Aristide Broussard, who was Perrin's great-grandfather and who leased the land to Chevron back in 1942.

The case has received significant play in the state and national media, and some important issues were settled in court that day, mostly in favor of the Broussard heirs. But it has dragged on so long—it was first filed in 1997—that no one but the main parties are paying attention any more. (And not all of them either. I was the only spectator in court, and when I met Perrin's wife and niece later that day, they hadn't even known there'd been a hearing.)

"Aristide started out with a horse and a saddle, he was a cattleman and raised pigs," Miguez remarked. "But he owned the land that Texaco needed. He only got a small share of the royalties, but it was a lot of money back then. The checks he got, it was hard to find a bank to cash them."

Aristide Broussard leased the land to Chevron (then Texaco) to build a gas-processing plant to produce airplane fuel for the World War II effort. Chevron also produced oil at the site, and over the years began piping in gas from offshore. Perrin and other family members, who span six generations, allege that Chevron, and other oil companies it subleased to, systematically damaged the property. The Broussards' experts estimated that the cost of fully cleaning up an eighty-acre property the family owned would be $300 million.

The Broussard heirs also had a second case going against Chevron, this one with national implications and which was before the US Fifth Circuit Court of Appeals in New Orleans. Though Chevron's processing plant and other operations shut down long ago, it still uses the property and maintains equipment there for moving gas to and from the so-called Henry Hub, which sits on neighboring land.

The Hub, which is operated by a Chevron subsidiary, sits at the intersection of various oil and natural gas pipeline systems. So much natural gas moves through the area that the Hub plays a key role in setting spot and future prices. Chevron has sued to expropriate it under eminent domain, citing the Hub's importance to national energy and security concerns.

A 2011 *New York Times* story about the lawsuit noted that disputes between pipeline operators and property owners are common, but added that the eminent-domain lawyers it spoke with had never heard of a comparable situation. Gideon Kanner, a professor emeritus at Loyola Law School in Los Angeles described Chevron's efforts to seize the land on national-security grounds as "a sui generis case."

The New Orleans firm of Smith Stag represents Perrin and the other Broussard heirs. Stuart Smith, who handled the Grefer case against Exxon, began filing legacy lawsuits in Mississippi in the 1980s and, after the state supreme court shut down the cases there, moved his practice to Louisiana. He has won a number of big judgments, and now spends a fair amount of time sailing the Caribbean on his eighty-foot yacht.[16]

Mike Stag, his partner, couldn't be in Abbeville in court that day because he had a bad cold, but when I saw him in New Orleans a few days later he gave me a stack of documents about the case. There was a deposition from a former Texaco employee, Randall Landry, who said it was company policy to "dispose" of oil wastes in pits on the property; internal corporate reports on a 1985 fire and explosion that forced the evacuation and temporary closure of the plant; a 1993 DEQ inspection report that noted "dead, moribund" fish inside a basin on the property; and documents alleging that cooling tower water—which contained high levels of chromium, a rust inhibitor—had migrated into the Boston Canal, a drainage bayou that runs through plant land and empties into Vermilion Bay to the south.

Miguez, the son of cotton sharecroppers, was born in 1950 and has lived in Abbeville all his life. Before heading to Perrin's land he gave me a rapid-fire tour of the town. We passed Depuy's Oyster Shop ("The same family's owned it since 1869; it's the best restaurant in town."); Planters Mill ("They make the best rice you'll ever eat and ship it all over the world."), Steen's Syrup Mill ("They make A-1 molasses. It's the main ingredient in Bullseye Masterpiece barbeque sauce, which is the best there is."), then drove out of town, past farms and rice fields that were covered in a foot of water for raising crawfish, it being off-season for rice.

Miguez chatted all along the way, about hunting muskrat and alligator, his preferred method of cooking gumbo, and hauling whiskey when he worked as a truck driver: "I'd pick it up in Bowling Green, Kentucky, in bulk, uncut; it was 190 proof and hotter than gasoline. You could light wet logs with it. Then I'd take it to Los Angeles, California, to be distilled to 80 percent. I picked it up from Jack Daniels in Kentucky, and when it came out in a bottle in California it was Old Grand Dad."

He drove me around the perimeter of the Broussard family property, a perfect square in the neighboring town of Erath. On it were rusty abandoned buildings, including the old gas plant, storage tanks, and a thin pipeline that brought natural gas from the Henry Hub to a rail rack three miles away, where it shipped out by train. "There used to be wells all over here," Miguez said as he pointed out the window. "I found some of the waste pits that contaminated the property, but they're all buried now."

At first glance, and some might say a second, it was hard to understand how the Broussards could have been asking for so much money from Chevron. Save for the rusted-out buildings, the setting looked bucolic, with cows lazing in a pasture and ducks swimming on ponds next door to the property. From there we drove to Erath's three-room Acadian Museum, which Perrin founded, runs, and uses as his law office when he's not working in Lafayette, his main residence. The museum has an eclectic collection—there's a Sears and Roebuck catalog from 1900, a painting of the Marquis de Lafayette, and an old wall-mounted hand-crank telephone that still works, which Miguez demonstrated by calling it from his cell phone—but is dedicated to honoring the Cajun heritage and people.

Perrin showed me around the museum, leading me to a framed facsimile of an apology issued by Queen Elizabeth for the British expulsion of Acadians from present-day Canada during the French and Indian War. Some of them, like Perrin's forebears, settled in Louisiana, where they became known as Cajuns. "In 1990 I heard about the US government offering an apology to Japanese-Americans interned during World War II," Perrin told me. "That led me to sue the Queen. Thirteen years later we worked out a deal, and she issued this apology."

We sat down in Perrin's small, cluttered office, where campaign posters for Huey Long and Jimmy Carter shared

wall space with the flags of New Brunswick and Nova
Scotia. Aristide Broussard, Perrin explained, never went to
school or learned to read. He originally leased the eighty
acres to Texaco for seventy-five years at sixteen hundred
dollars a year, a pittance even back in the 1940s. After he
graduated from law school, Perrin renegotiated the lease,
which still expires in 2018 but now pays his family about
one hundred thousand dollars annually, in line with typical
rates. The middlemen who got the lease for Texaco fleeced
Aristide as well on the issue of royalty payments for oil and
gas production on the property. Typically the landowner
received a royalty rate of one eighth, but the middlemen
convinced him to sell seven eighths of his share, leaving
him with one sixty-fourth, for thirty thousand dollars.
That was a lot of money in 1942 but cost Aristide and his
heirs many millions of dollars over the following decades.
"The middlemen knew what was underground and Aristide
didn't," Perrin said. "He had no idea of the people he was
dealing with."

Even so, Perrin maintained a good relationship with
Texaco over the years. He only sued the company and a
subleaser, Hilcorp, after learning that those two were
embroiled in a lawsuit of their own over mutual allegations
of mismanagement of operations at the family property. "I
learned about the damages to our property in the lawsuit
between the companies," he told me. "They were destroying the place; they nearly blew up the gas plant. We own
about three thousand acres, and I always represented the
family, but for a case like this I needed outside help, which
is how Mike and Stuart got involved."

The Broussard heirs settled with Hilcorp in November 2012, but Chevron had always denied having polluted Perrin's land and continued to fight the lawsuit. Sabine, the Chevron subsidiary that operates Henry Hub, offered to buy the property for $1 million. When Aristide's heirs rejected the offer, the company shifted to try eminent domain. "Aristide wanted that land maintained as a unit because he and his wife struggled so hard to get it, and he wanted his family to stay together," said Perrin. "How many people know their fifth cousins?"

"Seizing private land is a serious matter," he added. "It's not supposed to be done to put an end to a $300 million lawsuit against you." "We're not anti-oil," he added. "We're against companies that don't clean up their shit."

In mid-2013, just as the legacy lawsuit trial was about to begin, Chevron made a settlement offer (though it continued to deny responsibility for polluting the land). The two sides were also seeking to negotiate an end to the eminent-domain case. As of this writing, the talks between the parties had not concluded.

River traffic on the Mississippi at Baton Rouge consists mostly of barges, but an occasional oil tanker slides by as it heads to unload at a massive twenty-one-hundred-acre ExxonMobil refinery that processes over half a million barrels of crude oil daily and belches black clouds from its smokestacks around the clock. It's the fourth-largest refinery in the Unites States—second only to one the company operates in Texas—and sits near downtown and adjacent to a poor neighborhood called Standard Heights. The refinery has repeatedly been cited for violations of the Clean Air Act, which is a major reason that the EPA cited Baton Rouge for failing to meet federal ozone standard requirements between 1997 and 2011.

On June 14, 2012, residents of Standard Heights told Anna Hyrbyk, an environmental activist with a group called the Louisiana Bucket Brigades that works in the neighborhood, that a foul smell was emanating from the refinery. Hyrbyk e-mailed Esteban Herrera of the EPA—who was finally in town to visit the plant, in response to repeated complaints from the Bucket Brigades—and Cheryl Sonnier Nolan at the DEQ to let them know. Nolan e-mailed back to say that initial reports indicated a release of the carcinogen benzene, but that it was only ten pounds—the unit of measurement for chemical emissions—and that "air monitoring did not indicate levels of concern." Herrera e-mailed back, "As always you guys are on top of it."

The story would have ended there, but Hyrbyk kept after the regulators because neighborhood residents complained about headaches and a continuing stench from the plant. Exxon subsequently admitted that the benzene release was three thousand times higher than what Nolan had estimated. When I was in Baton Rouge in March 2013, the DEQ was holding hearings on a proposed air permit modification at the refinery that would allow benzene production to increase by 20 percent. Despite opposition from neighborhood residents, the increase was later approved.

The other dominant structure on the Baton Rouge skyline is the Louisiana State Capitol Building, which is located just about a mile away from the refinery. It was built by Huey Long in 1931 and resembles a smaller version of the Empire State Building, and at 450 feet and 34 stories is still the nation's tallest capital building. Green-uniformed inmates from the Dixon Correctional Institute tend to the immaculately kept grounds. At the heart of the complex is a statue of Long atop a marble pedestal, with an inscription that reads: "An unconquered friend of the poor who dreamed of the day when the wealth of the land would be spread among all the people."

I stopped by the capitol to interview Republican Senator Gerald Long, chairman of the Natural Resources Committee and a third cousin to Huey, second to Earl, first to Gillis Long, a former US congressman, and brother of Jimmy Long, who served thirty-two years in the state legislature. Long's basement office was decorated with a variety of family memorabilia, including a picture of dozens of Longs at their 1998 reunion in Winfield, where the clan originated.

The Longs are known for their passionate politics, but with Gerald, who wore a brown jacket with a gold and silver tie, the bloodline appears to have thinned. He won office as a senator in 2007 at the age of sixty-three, after working for decades as a State Farm agent. "You get one of these if you're one of the top fifty agents for State Farm out of seventeen thousand nationwide," he said proudly when I asked him about a big gold-and-diamond ring he had on. "I was one of the top fifty agents five different times."

I'd asked Long for an interview because a contact on the trial lawyer side told me he was sympathetic to the landowners' point of view, but it was impossible to get him to take a position on legacy lawsuits, either pro or con. "I've tried to stay neutral," he said. "The problem is that everyone thinks you're on the other side. If you come back in ten years, we may still be trying to settle this."

Long told me he favored giving industry "as many incentives as it needs," because Louisiana was driven by energy. "In my personal life I'm driven more by my lord and savior, Jesus Christ," said Long, who is a Baptist minister. "That is my faith, and I hope my commitment to my faith can be seen in my politics."

"I love being a senator," he continued on. "I may sit down with a CEO and then get a call from a little old lady who needs help in my district." There was clearly no point in continuing the conversation, and Long in any case was about to meet with a CEO, Ted Grabowski, of the Houston-based Texas Brine, the company responsible for the massive sinkhole at Bayou Corne. It took Long's committee six months to hold its first hearing after the disaster, and it was only at the end of March 2013 that Jindal finally traveled to Bayou Corne to meet with families. That visit finally occurred after angry residents spoke out in the press about the governor's lackadaisical response.

As I was getting ready to leave, Long told me, "You should speak to Senator Adley, he's the real architect of the legacy legislation. He's in the oil and gas business and understands it."

As luck had it, I already had an interview with Senator Adley set up for a few days later. Like Long, Adley is a Christian minister, but he is made of decidedly tougher stuff. When his secretary took me into his office he was on the phone with Don Briggs. I only heard his side of the conversation, but it was clear they were talking about legacy lawsuits, and Ginger Sawyer's name was mentioned a few times.

When he got off the phone, Adley, a plump, balding man of sixty-five who lives in the small town of Benton in northwest Louisiana, immediately asked me what I thought about legacy lawsuits. "I don't care, I'll tell you the same thing anyway; I just want to know where you stand," he said. And it certainly didn't seem to bother him, nor affect what he told me, when I let him know that my sympathies were generally on the landowners' side.

Adley sat at a neat wooden desk and chewed gum as we talked. I asked him about a picture on the wall of a young girl, his granddaughter as it turned out, who was sitting on a football field surrounded by an LSU helmet, football, and banner. "My wife was a featured twirler at LSU, and she bleeds purple and gold. Let me show you the present I gave her for Valentine's Day. It's a picture of her when she was a twirler; it ran on the front page of the *Advocate* in 1970," he said, as he showed me an image on his purple-and-gold-encased iPhone. "That's a two-by-three-foot oil painting I had done from the picture. She got mad at me; she said, 'Why'd you give me something that reminds me of what I looked like back then?' But now she has it hanging with a light on it."

When I asked Adley how important oil and gas were to the state, he said the better question was how important they were to the nation. "This country runs on energy," he said. "Industry in this state and other oil-producing states provides this energy to America. Every state offers something. My friends in Florida have their white sand beaches and Kansas offers agricultural crops. We provide energy."

When it came to legacy lawsuits, Adley said that he looked at the issue as a taxpayer and a citizen, not as an oilman, though he'd been one his entire life. "Protecting property rights is sacred to Republicans, but this issue is more complicated than that," he told me. "This is about harm to our state as a whole. You have trial lawyers who want to make money and oil companies who want to save money, and we elected officials have to divide the baby."

The oil industry made a big push to squelch legacy suits in 2006, three years after the Corbello ruling. "Money was being thrown around by both sides," Adley recalled with a shake of his head. "It's one of the few times I carried a weapon around here—I have a concealed-weapons permit."

That year, the oil lobby managed to push through, by a narrow margin, a bill that appeared to mark a significant step toward its goal of getting legacy suits out of the courts and into the hands of regulators. The new law restricted the right of judges and juries to set damage awards, gave the DNR greater authority to determine the extent of the cleanup required, and specified that companies would be allowed to recover any money left over from clean-up funds they were required by remediation plans to establish. "At that point we thought we'd won," said Adley. "But lo and behold, the trial attorneys got around that."[17]

The oil industry subsequently made other attempts to crack down further on legacy cases, and 2012 marked its biggest and most aggressive effort. The campaign kicked off one week before the spring legislative session opened when LMOGA and Exxon took Gerald Long and several of his committee staffers out to lunch at Sullivan's Steakhouse. On the day of the critical committee vote on the oil industry's bill, major landowners set up a command center in a senate conference room and tried furiously to kill the legislation. Meanwhile, oil-company officials and lobbyists worked with Adley out of his office to corral enough votes to pass it.

The committee passed the industry bill and it was subsequently approved by both houses of the legislature and signed by Jindal. A major change allows companies to avoid a trial by offering a limited admission of responsibility for pollution—but one not deemed an admission of legal guilt if subsequent litigation should arise—and go straight to the Conservation Office with a proposed clean-up plan. The other key change was that the bill stipulated that polluted land need only be cleaned to meet state regulatory standards, not restored "as nearly as possible" to its original condition, as had previously been the case. The oil lobby was pleased with the bill passed by the lawmakers. "When industry is able to work with the legislators and come to peaceful compromise, we get the opportunity to see our democracy at work," Briggs told the local press at the time.

Adley also expressed satisfaction with the outcome. "There's no question you can drive around Louisiana and see places where the oil and gas companies operated that need to be cleaned up," he told me. "But we'd become a playground for people who want to make money. We've regulated this industry. Louisiana has done a better job than most places, and certainly better than the federal government. BP was not on our watch, that's the feds. We've never had problems like that."

"The government sets the rules and regulations on the oil industry," he added. "If you don't like them, get your elected officials to change them."

Which makes perfect sense in a high school civics textbook but is not a realistic option in industry-friendly Louisiana.

Despite the new restrictions passed by the legislature in 2012, hundreds of legacy cases remain to be settled, and about two dozen new ones have been filed since that year's bill was passed. On my last night in Baton Rouge, I met Mike Veron, another prominent trial lawyer, at Sullivan's Steakhouse, the same spot where LMOGA had wined and dined Senator Long and committee staffers.[18] Two other lawyers and a paralegal from his firm accompanied him; they'd flown in on a private plane from Shreveport, where they'd taken depositions for an upcoming case, and after dinner would continue home to Lake Charles.

Veron had arranged a large private room off the lobby that Sullivan's uses on weekends as a club, with a DJ and dancing. The room had a screen to show a PowerPoint presentation Veron's firm had prepared. Tall, well built, and with neatly groomed short hair, Veron looks "establishment," as he put it, and for a long time he was, spending a quarter-century as a defense attorney for the oil industry.

"I recovered huge amounts of money for them in two cases, and my bonus above the hourly rate was a box of golf balls," he told me as we sat on bar stools while his team worked to get the PowerPoint up and running. "That's when I decided it might be better to work on contingency and came over from the dark side or, depending on who you're talking to, went over to the dark side."

Veron is the lawyer who won the Corbello case against Shell; William Corbello hired him because they were cousins. "We found documents in that case that blew me away," Veron said, taking a sip of scotch. "I thought I'd never see a case with documents like that again, but every one of them has them. Now I expect it."

Rock Palermo, a lawyer with Veron's firm and the plane pilot, had joined us. "There are two truisms," he said. "First, when there are oil and gas operations, there is bound to be environmental damage. Second, we'll find memos that show they knew exactly what they were doing."

We moved to a long table in the center of the room and ordered dinner: steaks, creamed spinach, sautéed mushrooms, and a bottle of red wine. "I defended asbestos manufacturers when I was on the dark side, and I won a few cases, by the way," Veron said. "The whole issue with toxicity is, you're dealing with dosage. Two aspirin are great for a headache, but if you take the whole bottle, it will cause internal hemorrhaging. We sprinkle salt on our food, but a shakerful of it all at once will kill a child."

The PowerPoint presentation commenced as we waited for the food, and Veron used a red laser pointer to highlight key facts and images as the slides played. They told the story of a recent case, M. J. Farms Ltd. v. Exxon et al., in which Veron's firm had won an undisclosed settlement. In 2005, brothers Ron and Michael Johnson bought the property—at forty-six square miles, it would be the state's fifth-biggest city by area—which had previously been used for farming and oil production, sometimes simultaneously. Veron shook his head as photographs taken on the property of a large salt scar, barren marshes, and corroded pipelines flashed by on the screen.

We broke briefly as a waitress served the food, after which Veron's narration and the PowerPoint resumed. For decades Exxon and other companies who leased the land had collectively produced an estimated thirty-two million barrels of oil and many multiples more of brine. Large quantities of it leached into the soil and groundwater from unlined pits and poorly maintained saltwater injection wells.

Internal corporate documents from back in 1959 show that an Exxon predecessor firm was considering spending $7,400 to upgrade an old injection well but decided against it because "of the relatively large expenditure required." Instead it opted to continue using the well "until we are forced to shut [it] because of excessive damage claims or because of orders from the Conservation Commission. After shutting in the well, an attempt should be made to sell the well, and if this is not possible the well should be abandoned."

Exxon claimed at trial that the water on the property was "naturally salty," though its own soil scientist testified under oath that he was "99.9 percent sure" that the contamination was caused by brine from oil and gas operations. In 1982, corporate documents show, Exxon disposed of 547,415 barrels of salt water into an "open hole." A DEQ inspection report of the property six years later said that "unpermitted saltwater discharges" had been "a chronic problem at this facility in the past."

"This was not the Middle Ages," said Veron, whose untouched steak had gone cold. "In a rational state, someone goes to jail for this type of behavior."

In January 2013, the Louisiana Supreme Court ruled in Vermilion Parish School Board v. Louisiana Land and Exploration Company that if a judge or jury concluded that a lease contained an implied obligation to restore the land to above the regulatory standard, that can be ordered. That decision terrified the industry and is the one Ginger Sawyer was referring to when she told me she had a lawmaker lined up to introduce a bill to remedy it if the supreme court failed to rehear the case and reverse itself.

"Every time there's talk in the legislature about increasing taxes or regulation on the companies, or the courts hold them accountable for their actions, the industry threatens to leave Louisiana," Veron said as we were leaving Sullivan's. "The truth is, they drill here because there's oil here, so why are we giving it all away and letting them destroy the environment?"

So as the legislative session opened in 2013, the industry in Louisiana was keeping a close eye on legacy lawsuit politics. At the national level, its chief concern was the EPA's ongoing study of future rules on shale fracking. Briggs has already said that his association would be working with elected officials to lobby for continued state control of fracking rules, and he warns that the EPA, if given a greater role, "could shut the domestic industry down if some company somewhere makes one mistake."

It certainly wouldn't be the first time Louisiana politicians and businesses played a key role in winning protection for the oil industry from federal regulations on human health and the environment. An earlier group of Louisianans, led by Senator J. Bennett Johnston and Representative (and future senator) John Breaux successfully mounted the industry's defense against calls for tough new environmental regulations that arose after the exposure in the mid-1970s of the Love Canal disaster.[19]

In a little-known and long-forgotten story,[20] the Comprehensive Environmental Response, Compensation and Liability Act (CERCLA) began to make its way through Congress in the spring of 1980. The bill, which sought to establish rules on liability and the cleanup of toxic spills and releases, included a list of hazardous substances to be covered by the statute. Of four competing House bills, three put oil and gas waste on that list. President Jimmy Carter signed the final bill that emerged from negotiations on December 11, 1980. Thanks to industry lobbying, it specifically exempted crude oil and petroleum—even though benzene, toluene, xylene, and ethylbenzene, all of which are contained in petroleum waste, were listed.

Four years earlier, Congress had enacted the Resource Conservation and Recovery Act (RCRA), which empowered the EPA to regulate hazardous wastes. In 1978, when it published its first set of standards in the Federal Register, the EPA proposed an exemption, pending further review, for supposedly less toxic "special wastes," and included oil and gas waste in that category.

By 1979, the EPA was leaning toward overturning the petroleum exemption. Industry lobbyists "stormed" the EPA to oppose that, according to an article published on March 19 of that year in the *Oil and Gas Journal*. "Several groups said inclusion of these substances among waste materials considered hazardous would be 'devastating' to the oil and gas industry," the article said. "They urged EPA to suspend regulation of industry waste materials until studies of the materials are completed."

In October 1980, Congress passed legislation that maintained the oil and gas exemption and kept petroleum wastes off RCRA's section C, which requires the most stringent regulations, and put them under subtitle D, which covers "nonhazardous wastes" that are monitored much more loosely. Congress directed EPA to conduct a study on the hazardous nature of oil and gas wastes and report its findings. EPA didn't begin work on the study until 1985, when a small nonprofit group, the Alaska Center for the Environment, won a lawsuit that forced it to comply.

EPA finally issued its report on December 28, 1987, and it identified various hazards posed by oil and gas waste, including danger to human health from consuming fish and shellfish contaminated by groundwater polluted with seepage from storage and disposal pits. Seven months later, following a second round of intense lobbying by the oil and gas industry, the EPA issued a regulatory determination to Congress. An accompanying report identified poor industry disposal practices, inadequate regulations, and public health risks posed by oil field waste. Brine, it said, could contain toxic constituents, including fluoride, lead, cadmium, arsenic, benzene, and barium, at levels one hundred times greater than "health-based standards."

Nonetheless, the EPA concluded that regulation of oil and gas waste was "not warranted" and that existing state regulations were more than adequate.

A 1989 *Times-Picayune* story estimated that oil companies collectively saved $6.7 billion annually with their CERCLA and RCRA exemptions. "This exemption does not make sense from an environmental perspective," an EPA enforcement official told the newspaper. "This country runs on petroleum, and the oil interests in Congress are extremely powerful. They wanted the exemption. They got the exemption."[21]

And over the years they got many more. All told the industry enjoys significant exemptions from numerous environmental statutes, including the Clean Water Act, the Safe Drinking Water Act, the Clean Air Act, and the National Environmental Policy Act—the "Magna Carta" of environmental legislation passed in 1970. The Oil Pollution Act approved by Congress in the wake of the Exxon Valdez spill capped civil liability for oil companies at $75 million. Efforts to raise that figure to $75 billion after the BP Horizon spill were blocked in the Senate, with Louisiana Democrat Mary Landrieu leading the resistance.

"It's terribly difficult to get beyond denial, that's the first step, and the big agony," Oliver Houck told me when we met in New Orleans. "But they've known all along what harm they were doing and ignored it, just like the tobacco industry and nuclear industry and asbestos manufacturers. The BP disaster was quite a blow. It makes it hard for them to say that industry is being unfairly persecuted by a bunch of greedy trial lawyers, and it resurrected the idea that tort law is a needed supplement to government regulation."

When it comes to legacy lawsuits, the industry is surely more than a little disingenuous when it argues that it used unlined pits and discharged brine into coastal waters only when it was legal to do so, and hence the companies did nothing wrong. It is true that it was legal to store waste in unlined pits up until 1986, but it wasn't legal if the pits leaked and contaminated the land. It was legal to discharge salt water into coastal waters with a permit, but the companies frequently did so without getting one. Furthermore, Louisiana's weak environmental rules and enforcement resulted in large part from intense industry pressure on politicians and regulatory agencies that it essentially owned.

At this point in time, corporations have so much power at the state and federal level that the trial lawyers, whatever their personal and collective flaws, are the only force left in America to challenge and hold them accountable. And even if the Louisiana oil industry's worst charges are true, that the trial lawyers are unscrupulous ambulance chasers primarily interested in self-enrichment, it is still indisputably certain that they "pillaged" the land, as their ally Senator Morrell put it, and that they knew what they were doing and did it anyway, because it saved them money. The evidence for that is in the companies' own files and scattered and buried all across the state of Louisiana.

7

Coda: The Hustler: Neil Bush

Whatever one's opinions of the politics or actions of the figures profiled in this book, most of them (I would specifically exclude Teodorin Obiang here) are formidable figures that flourished on the basis of intelligence, enterprise, charm, or a combination of such traits. But even more than most industries—perhaps because, as in the arms business, the financial payoff for closing even a single big deal can be so huge—the energy business attracts a relatively large number of con artists and hangers-on. Those in the latter category may not have any discernible talents but are able to thrive nonetheless due to their proximity to powerful, well-connected people.

Consider, for example, the case of Neil Bush.

The American oil industry, and indeed the entire global energy industry, owes an enormous debt of gratitude to the Bush family for years of faithful service promoting its general and specific interests. Which is the only imaginable reason that US and foreign energy firms continue to seek Neil's services.

The son of one president and brother of another, Neil's political clout has declined since Barack Obama replaced George W. Bush in 2009. Two decades ago, the *Washington Post* observed that his business ventures had "a history of crashing and burning in spectacular fashion," and time, alas, seems not to have improved his record. Neil claims to have thirty years in the energy industry, though at least ten people from the Texas oil patch I spoke with said they had never heard of him playing any notable role in the energy business. Of the former first sibling one international oil executive and consultant told me, "I can't imagine anything he could bring to the table."

Yet Bush, who declined to speak with me, seems to have no trouble staying busy and prosperous. Chinese firms hire him to try to open doors in Africa, and US companies retain him to do the same in Central Asia. Neil is also the founder and CEO of a number of small energy companies—it's not clear exactly what they do or if he has financial backers—and lives a life of ease and comfort in Houston, where he resides with his second wife in a luxury condo and regularly graces the social pages.

He travels far in search of deals. As the chairman of Houston-based TX Oil, Neil met with Turkmenistan's dictator, Gurbanguly Berdimuhamedov, in an effort to gain offshore oil concessions in the Caspian Sea. The tightly controlled state media claimed that he brought a letter from former president George H. W. Bush wishing Berdimuhamedov "sound health and successes" and thanking him for inviting Neil "to your beautiful country and for receiving him personally despite your heavy workload."

In November 2010, Neil returned to the country for the Turkmenistan International Oil and Gas Conference, and TX Oil hosted the event's closing cocktail party. "The oil business is in the Bush family bloodline," he declared, according to an account in an energy industry publication, *Nefte Compass*.

Not everyone seemed happy about Bush's potential involvement in Turkmenistan. A story in *News Central Asia* said:

> It is the eastern tradition to receive all guests with open arms. However, as independent observers we would recommend that the government of Turkmenistan should consider carefully before committing to any proposals brought by Neil Bush. For one thing, [his company] is a virtually unknown entity … On top of that, he has a history of questionable business practices.

Predictably, Neil's efforts to secure concessions in the country ended in failure.

Neil first distinguished himself when the Silverado Savings and Loan of Denver went belly-up in 1988 at a time when his father was finishing a second term as Ronald Reagan's vice president. While serving on the S&L's board of directors, Neil voted to approve $100 million in loans to two of his business partners—he somehow neglected to mention these relationships to fellow board members—who both subsequently went bankrupt. This adventure in socialized capitalism cost US taxpayers $1.3 billion.

One of the loan recipients was JNB International, an energy exploration company Neil founded with one hundred dollars out of his own pocket and somewhat larger sums from two Denver real estate moguls. "Tell him Neil Bush called," he reportedly told a secretary when leaving a message for a Denver oilman during this period. "You know, the vice president's son."

The family safety net spared Neil from the full consequences of his misdeeds. In regard to Silverado, federal investigators found "breaches of his fiduciary duties involving multiple conflicts of interest." The younger Bush was banned from banking and ordered to pay a fifty-thousand-dollar fine at a civil trial, but a Republican fundraiser held on his behalf helped ease the sting of settling that debt.

Neil went on to found a gas-exploration company called Apex Energy with $2.3 million from Bush-family friend Louis Marx Jr. Neil, who put up $3,000 of his own money, received $300,000 in salary over the next two years, at which point Apex went broke. Little gas was ever found. Next up came a brief stint at TransMedia Communications, owned by a cable TV baron who had raised more than $300,000 for George H. W. Bush. Neil's annual pay was $60,000 and his job description was daunting: "learn the business." In 1993, two years after the conclusion of the first Gulf War, the emir of Kuwait flew Bush Sr. over on his private plane for a ceremony honoring him for leading the coalition that evicted Saddam Hussein. Neil and former secretary of state James Baker traveled along to try to arrange a power plant deal for Enron, which never happened.

The post-Silverado years proved dark for Neil, so it was fortunate that another family friend, Jamal Daniel, stepped in to help out. A Syrian-American fixer with substantial interests in the international energy business and beyond, Daniel has close ties to the ruling families in Saudi Arabia, Qatar, Syria, Lebanon, and Yemen.

Daniel lives in Houston and was a major donor to the presidential campaigns of both Bush Sr. and Bush Jr., and to the latter's 1994 Texas gubernatorial campaign. In 2003, after the invasion of Iraq, he and other Bush administration cronies set up New Bridge Strategies LLC to advise companies seeking business in post-Saddam Iraq. The consulting firm didn't work out so well—probably because few businesses cared to invest in war-torn Iraq—though the Paris-based newsletter *Intelligence Online* reported in 2011 that Daniel had invested in an oil deal in Iraqi Kurdistan, so the invasion wasn't a total loss for him. (There is no indication that Neil had any role in the investment.)

Daniel treats Neil like next of kin. Over the years he has paid for Neil's family to take a trip to Disneyland Paris and bought Neil and his first wife, Sharon, a $380,000 cottage in Maine. Neil also married his second wife, Maria, at Daniel's Houston mansion.

In return, Neil has occasionally exerted himself. Back in the late 1990s Daniel made Neil cochairman of Crest Investment Corporation and paid him $60,000 annually for a few hours of work per week. Separately, Daniel and other Bush family friends financially backed Neil's education company, Ignite! Much of the firm's business was obtained through sole-source contracts from school districts in Texas. In 2006, his mother donated an undisclosed amount of money to the Bush-Clinton Katrina Fund with specific instructions that it be earmarked to buy

Ignite! products for local schools that took in hurricane evacuees.

Yet for all the handouts from the Bush family network, Neil's ventures still failed to generate much profit. His famously nasty 2003 divorce proceedings with Sharon revealed that he was essentially broke. At the time, a well-placed source told me, he drove a minivan owned by his mother. The proceedings also revealed that on at least three business trips to Asia, women Neil didn't know came into his hotel room unbidden and had sex with him. The practice, he acknowledged, seemed "very unusual."

"You don't think he was picked to be part of all of those business deals because he was so brilliant, do you?" Marshall Davis Brown, Sharon Bush's attorney, asked when I met him at his Houston office. "He had a big hat but no horse."

Neil has received relatively little press attention since his divorce, though he has been living well. In February 2005, Mexican magnate Jaime Camil hosted a fiftieth birthday party for Neil at his estate in Acapulco. The *Houston Chronicle* reported that two-dozen Houstonians flew down for the festivities. "Saturday night, the host-with-the-most pulled out the stops at his expansive villa," wrote the newspaper's society columnist. "A lavish fireworks display topped off a night that included a 16-piece mariachi band, dancers from Mexico City's Ballet Folklorico and gourmet fare."

The truth is, failure has been very good to Neil. He currently resides in a $1.6 million, six-bedroom, five-bathroom condominium located near Houston's upscale West

Oaks Mall. He has in recent years set up at least ten firms in Houston and Austin, according to incorporation records filed with the Texas secretary of state's office. His companies have generic names like GCC Source Point, Global XS2, BTZ Holdings, and ATX Oil, and it's hard to find out much about them, since they are registered as limited liability companies (and hence little public disclosure is required), mostly don't have Web sites, and almost never turn up in news accounts. If he has consummated any deals through these firms, they were probably not big.

One of Neil's firms is registered at an address that doesn't exist, and several are registered at his condo, including a firm called Nexus Energy, which actually operates from (or at least has an office at) an oil firm headed by his current wife's ex-husband, Robert Andrews. Neil established Nexus in late 2008 "to pursue business opportunities both overseas and in the United States," according to a corporate profile it has distributed. "[Neil has] cultivated many relationships among private business people and large energy-related enterprises in Asia and the Middle East. Nexus seeks to leverage these relationships to act on behalf of a client or partner company." In November 2009, Neil represented Nexus at an energy conference in New Orleans, at which Karl Rove tagged along.

Firms from China regularly retain Neil, which isn't surprising given the deep ties his family has there. Bush Sr. was appointed as US liaison in Beijing under President Gerald Ford, and during his presidency sought greatly expanded trade with Beijing while downplaying human rights concerns. George W. Bush also forged a close relationship with

China, and Neil's deceased uncle, Prescott Bush Jr., was a close friend of former premier Jiang Zemin and did a good deal of business there.

In March 2013, Bush Sr., wife Barbara, and Neil had dinner at the residence of the Chinese consul general in Houston. The Chinese government expressed hope in a written statement that the Bushes would "continue playing an important role in making contributions to ... the friend-ship between the two peoples." For their part the Bush family said the visit felt "like home" and expressed special pleasure at being served "their favorite Beijing Roasted Duck." The consul general and the Bushes also "exchanged views on China–US relations ... and other issues of their common interest."

These sorts of ties have surely contributed to Neil's list of Chinese clients, mainly companies seeking natural resource deals in Africa, including Shougang Holdings, a state-owned steel giant. In 2009, Neil led a delegation of the company's officials to Liberia, where Shougang was seeking an iron ore mining concession. The Neil connec-tion didn't help: An Israeli firm ultimately won out.

The same year Neil traveled to Ghana with executives from oil giant Sinopec, the world's seventh-largest firm and a major competitor of US companies. Neil managed to get meetings with top local political leaders. A source familiar with Bush's efforts said that he opened doors in Ghana with the help of his friend Chris Wilmot, a busi-nessman originally from Ghana who now lives in Houston. "Chris has the ties in Ghana that go all the way to the top," this person told me. "Neil was riding on his coattails over there." To no avail. Neil's clients didn't get the deal they were angling for.

On a weekday morning in 2011, I stopped by TX Oil's headquarters in a bland office building on Westheimer Road in Houston. New Age music played from a Bose system in the reception area, which was decorated with a cowboy painting, an aquarium, and a leather sofa. The office wasn't bristling with activity, and the secretary told me no one would be available to talk to me about TX Oil.

"Is there a brochure or any information you can give me?" I asked.

"Not yet," she replied with a cool smile.

In late 2013, Neil turned up in suburban Cincinnati, where two other companies he is involved with—American Pacific International Capital Inc. of Portland, Oregon and Singapore-based SingHaiyi Group[1]—had paid $45 million for the Tri-County Mall. The property, which had been in foreclosure, was sold at an auction by the local sheriff's office.

The local mayor, Doyle Webster, told WCPO TV that he hoped Bush's name would help bring in tenants to the mall. "He can certainly open up some doors," Webster was quoted as saying. "People are going to take his phone calls where they wouldn't take yours or mine." WCPO noted that the Bush family had "extensive political and business ties" in the area, and that Cincinnati was "home to three of the twenty most lucrative zip codes for George W. Bush in the 2000 presidential campaign." Neil, who was touring the mall, told the TV station that he had sought advice from several Cincinnati business leaders before making the investment. "They said their wives come to this mall," he said. "They come to this mall like six times a year. I said, 'It must be in a good neighborhood if my friends are coming here.'"

Why do companies keep hiring Neil? It can't be for his business acumen. More likely, his employers write checks out of friendship, loyalty, and interest in currying favor with his family's business and political network. In a reflection of the declining value of the Bush family name in the age of Obama, Neil does not seem to command the fees he once did.

In 2002, he received payments of $2 million in stock and $10,000 per board meeting from Grace Semiconductor—a firm backed by the son of Jiang Zemin—even though he knew nothing at all about semiconductors. In December 2012 he was named a director of China Timber Resources Group, which has forest resources in Guyana and China. Neil's director's fee was a mere $1,200 a month, which the company said "was determined with reference to his experience, scope of work, level of involvement, seniority, as well as the prevailing market conditions."

Ouch. It's tough to be a fixer who can't fix much, and yet for Neil Bush and other denizens of the secret world of oil, there will always be other opportunities.

Notes

1. The Fixers: Ely Calil

1 Or at least that's what he told me. By other accounts he was born in Germany, Austria, Turkey, or New Orleans.

2 Norway is considered one of the cleanest countries, but during the past decade Statoil, the state oil company, was caught paying bribes through middlemen to win major contracts, once in Iran and again in Libya. "Statoil offered the Iranians social programs, infrastructure, all sorts of benefits in exchange for the deal there, but the Iranians wanted money," said one person familiar with the arrangements. "The locals were not interested in the alternatives, and other competitors were happy to offer payments, so Statoil did what everyone else was doing: They used agents to make payments, and they did it in a ham-handed way and got caught."

3 The Senate report includes a memo that Citibank's Alain Ober, a private banking officer who handled Bongo's account, sent to several colleagues:

> I never asked our client where his money came from. My guess ... is that in view of the importance of our client's country as a provider of cheap oil to France, it was (and still is) important that our client stayed in power and thus the French government/French oil companies (Elf) made "donations" to him (very much like we give to PACs in the US!).

4   He sold Sloane House that year to Sir Anthony Bamford, chairman of a global construction-equipment firm, for an estimated £30 million (approximately $48 million).

5   Wade was voted out in 2012, leaving office amid widespread charges of corruption.

6   She is the widow of former president René Moawad, who was assassinated in a 1989 car bombing likely orchestrated by Syria.

7   In 1981, his ten-year-old son drowned in a swimming pool at the home of Prince Sultan Al-Saud. A fictionalized account of that story is told in the film *Syriana*.

2. The Dictators: Teodorin Obiang

1   Based on subsequent revelations about corruption in his country, Obiang's wealth surely stands in the billions by now.

2   Despite the US government's public commitment to keeping corrupt foreign officials out of the country, it appears to be reluctant to make use of 7750. The list of those banned under the proclamation is classified, but two confidential sources I spoke to said there are only about three dozen names on it. These include, according to a few foreign press accounts and the sources, officials from Cambodia, Kenya, and Nigeria.

3   In 2009, Jefferson was sentenced to thirteen years in prison on counts that included bribery and conspiracy to violate the Foreign Corrupt Practices Act. Several of the charges were related to his efforts to help companies win oil concessions in Equatorial Guinea.

4   A Texas oilman named William Lee founded Triton. He ran the firm until 1993, when charges surfaced that it had won favor in Indonesia by bribing government officials. Triton ultimately paid a $300,000 fine to settle the charges but denied any wrongdoing. The company then called Amerada Hess (it changed its name to Hess Corporation in 2006) bought Triton in 2001, primarily to acquire its Equatorial Guinea stake.

5   Levinson later represented the Iraqi National Congress, the exile group that led the push for the American invasion of Iraq on the basis of phony allegations about Saddam Hussein's stockpiles of WMDs and ties to Al Qaeda.

6   Wihbey's Institute was based in Israel, which of course had particular reasons to push the US away from Middle Eastern oil suppliers.

7   Riggs, which also did extensive business with former Chilean dictator Augusto Pinochet, was later hit with a $16 million fine for violations of the Bank Secrecy Act. It was subsequently sold to PNC Financial Services.

8   The Senate report also showed that oil companies paid for scholarships at American universities that went to children of Equatorial Guinea's leaders. The oil companies apparently still offer scholarship funding for Obiang relatives who attend universities in South Africa. ExxonMobil, Hess, and Marathon pay for clan members to attend universities in Johannesburg, Pretoria, and Cape Town, according to a Spanish academic who interviewed numerous Equatoguinean students in those cities. The academic did not know how much money the oil companies provided, but the students clearly lived well. This person met a nephew of Obiang's who rented an apartment at a luxury shopping mall in Pretoria and was known for his constant parties.

9   Berger and Nagler were outed as Teodorin's helpers in a 2010 Senate report, but even after that he was able to employ Americans to help him handle his financial and corporate affairs. At least until mid-2012 Teodorin retained the services of a little-known Los Angeles area accountant named James McCaleb. According to his Web site, McCaleb—who operates out of a business center in Pasadena and also has an office in Honolulu—and his firm help clients "concentrate all of your resources on what matters most; increasing revenues and reducing taxes." McCaleb serves as a director for several limited liability companies he incorporated for Teodorin—whose name does not appear anywhere on corporate records—including Malibu Estate Management LLC and Beautiful Vision. Teodorin's American financial wizard didn't have a stellar record when it came to his own finances. McCaleb filed for bankruptcy in 2008, listing debts of around $900,000, mostly to credit card companies, and savings of only $1,000 and $100 "cash on hand." McCaleb settled with his creditors in 2009 after receiving court-ordered credit counseling.

10   Various members of the Jackson family have done well from their acquaintance with Teodorin. Michael's brother, Marlon Jackson, reportedly visited Equatorial Guinea at his invitation to discuss potential agricultural deals.

11   In 2011, Davis ended his relationship with the Obiang regime and sued Equatorial Guinea after the government stiffed him for almost $142,000 worth of fees and expenses.

3. The Traders: Glencore

1 Volatility in 2012 was far less dramatic, but prices still ranged from a low of $90 per barrel to a high of $125, which by historical standards is still a lot of movement.

2 Of course, as Glencore grew it traded more and more commodities, but even at the time of the IPO, its oil trading division was the company's most profitable.

3 Like others, he would talk only on the condition that I not reveal his name.

4 International sanctions did not ban fuel sales to Damascus at the time, so they were not illegal, but they came amid calls by the US and some European governments for a boycott on energy deals with Syria.

5 In the US, freewheeling speculation in oil has its roots in the waning days of the Clinton administration. In December 2000 the president signed the Commodity Futures Modernization Act. The bill contained a provision, which came to be known as the Enron Loophole, that created a regulatory exemption for oil and "energy products" under the primary law regulating derivatives. Then senator Phil Gramm was the leading force behind this piece of legislation. His wife, Wendy Gramm, who served on the Commodity Futures Trading Commission under George W. Bush, pushed through rules that further eased regulation of energy speculation, and then took a job on Enron's board.

6 Glencore continued to do business with Iran after the 1979 Islamic revolution, and in recent years has been a regular supplier of gasoline to the country. It halted deliveries in late 2009 under pressure from the US government.

7 Clinton pardoned Green as well. In 2009, Green lived in Jerusalem and had a fortune of $1.2 billion, according to *Forbes* magazine, which ranked him no. 601 on its annual list of the world's richest people.

8 Cohen denies that they were undervalued.

9 Gertler's spokesman, Cohen, told me that his client had "never been personally engaged in business enterprises with Glencore." This turned out to be a rather flimsy distinction, for Cohen acknowledged that Gertler is "an adviser" to a private consulting company called Fleurette, registered in Gibraltar and "owned by a trust for the benefit of the Gertler family." Fleurette happens to have a "long-standing business relationship with Glencore."

4. The Gatekeepers: Bretton Sciaroni

1   Directly behind Cambodia were Pakistan (thirty-seven cents an hour), Vietnam (thirty-eight cents), and Sri Lanka (forty-three cents). China, with wages of between fifty-five and eighty cents per hour in inland areas, was the ninth cheapest.

2   The conventional wisdom in the US, among government officials, academics, and pundits, is that wages in the Third World are as high as they need to be. "Before Barack Obama and his team act on their talk about 'labor standards,' I'd like to offer them a tour of the vast garbage dump here in Phnom Penh," *New York Times* columnist Nicholas Kristof wrote back in 2008, in his inimitable prose style that resembles nothing so much as a den mother addressing a troop of Brownies. "The miasma of toxic stink leaves you gasping, breezes batter you with filth, and even the rats look forlorn ... Many families actually live in shacks on this smoking garbage." For families living in the dump, "a job in a sweatshop is a cherished dream, an escalator out of poverty," and attempts by Obama to push for "living wages" for apparel workers in the Third World would merely ratchet up production costs for industry and lead to factory shutdowns and layoffs. "The central challenge in the poorest countries," he wrote, "is not that sweatshops exploit too many people, but that they don't exploit enough." Incidentally, Kristof's speakers bureau, APB, says his typical fee is approximately $30,000. Hence, for an hour during which he offers "a compassionate glimpse" into global poverty and gives a "voice to the voiceless," as his APB profile puts it, Kristof pockets what a Cambodian apparel worker would make in about fifty years.

3   Sciaroni discussed the general political situation in Cambodia during our interview in Phnom Penh, but he declined to reply to subsequent questions about Iran–Contra and CALG or his current business or political activities.

4   A peace agreement between the government and the guerrillas was concluded in 1992, but the following year the Salvadoran Legislative Assembly, dominated by right-wing parties, adopted a blanket amnesty law that shielded all military and guerrilla forces from prosecution for human rights abuses committed during the war. In 1999, a report issued by the Inter-American Commission on Human Rights that discussed El Salvador's failure to prosecute those responsible for the Jesuits' massacre called the amnesty bill a violation of international law.

5   Foreign companies frequently make donations for "social" projects as a means of winning favor with senior officials. Cambodian government records show that in 2010 BHP donated an undisclosed amount of money to Hun Sen's personal bodyguard unit, Battalion E70, allegedly for humanitarian aid to the poor. In 2009, in a ceremony marking its fifteenth anniversary, Hun Sen described E70 as having made a "great contribution to the protection of national sovereignty and security of the people, and to the prevention of social unrests and terrorism." E70's true record is decidedly less benign. In 1997, opposition politician Sam Rainsy and about two hundred supporters gathered in a park across the street from the National Assembly in Phnom Penh to protest judicial corruption. A 1999 report by Human Rights Watch said:

> In a well-planned attack, four grenades were thrown into the crowd, killing protesters and bystanders, including children, and blowing limbs off street vendors. An FBI investigation concluded that Cambodian government officials were responsible for the attack. On the day of the grenade attack, Prime Minister Hun Sen's personal bodyguard unit, [Brigade E70], was, for the first time, deployed at a demonstration. The elite military unit, in full riot gear, not only failed to prevent the attack, but was seen by numerous witnesses opening up its lines to allow the grenade-throwers to escape and threatening to shoot people trying to pursuing the attackers.

No one was ever punished for the attack, and E70 has allegedly been involved in subsequent abuses, among them at natural resource concessions.

6   Though in January 2014 large protests, led by apparel workers, erupted in Phnom Penh, posing the first serious challenge to Hun Sen since he took power. His regime reacted in typical fashion: the violent eviction of protesters from a public square, a ban on all public gatherings, and security forces attacking striking workers, killing at least four of them. Opposition to Hun Sen had been brewing since the previous July, when his party claimed victory in elections that were widely seen as badly flawed. Two months later opposition leaders began threatening large strikes and protests, which Sciaroni dismissed. A September 2013 story in the *Cambodia Daily* said that, in Sciaroni's opinion, "savvy investors" would not be disturbed by strikes or protests. "Investors like political stability," he told the newspaper. "That has been a selling point for Cambodia."

5. The Flacks: Tony Blair

1   "Embassy monitors, who have attended nearly every session over the past year, have never seen her present in Parliament," the cable said.

2   Some five years later, Karimova launched a new line of attack in her charm offensive by bringing Sting to Uzbekistan for a concert and to accompany her to a "cultural festival" she sponsored. When attacked by critics, Sting, who was reportedly paid as much as $3 million for the trip, defended himself by saying that UNICEF had cosponsored the concert, which turned out to be false, and that while he was "well aware of the Uzbek president's appalling reputation in the field of human rights," he went to Uzbekistan anyway, because he had "come to believe that cultural boycotts are not only pointless gestures, they are counterproductive, where proscribed states are further robbed of the open commerce of ideas and art." The statement didn't specify whether Sting reached that conclusion before or after he cashed his check.

3   Papers found in Tripoli after Gaddafi's overthrow showed that Blair had even offered advice to his son Saif Gaddafi, now wanted for war crimes by the International Criminal Court, on his PhD thesis for the London School of Economics, "The Role of Civil Society in the Democratization of Global Governance Institutions."

4   There is zero evidence that Blair ever pushed Gaddafi to "reform" Libya's system. Evidence found in Tripoli after the dictator's fall shows that he was unfailingly polite with Gaddafi during their meetings and focused on business.

5   Blair's complex corporate setup "was done on legal and accountancy advice to preserve confidentiality, not to avoid tax as is sometimes maliciously suggested," spokeswoman Grant says.

6   The Kuwaitis have a long history of rewarding their friends against Saddam Hussein. They contributed heavily to the presidential library of George Bush Sr., the architect of Gulf War I, and various Bush family members and former administration officials won deals in Kuwait soon after that conflict.

7   This isn't the first time that Nazarbayev has used a Western intermediary to assemble a team of spin doctors to market his regime. Back in the late 1990s he spent $4 million to hire American lobbyists and PR consultants, among them Mark Siegel, a former Democratic National Committee executive

director, and Michael Deaver, a deputy chief of staff to President Reagan. That team was put together by James Giffen (see Chapter One), an American business consultant who funneled tens of millions of dollars to Nazarbayev out of fees Giffen received from oil companies that won stakes in Kazakh oil fields. During the same time, Gerald Carmen, a former US representative to the United Nations in Geneva under Ronald Reagan, was paid more than $1 million to help "establish President Nazarbayev as one of the foremost emerging leaders of the New World." As further thanks, Nazarbayev gifted Carmen a tasseled cap and a decorative whip.

8   David Plouffe, a former senior aide to Barack Obama, was paid fifty thousand dollars (from a pro-government group) for a speech he gave in Azerbaijan in 2009. After receiving a wave of criticism from local Azeri groups, he donated his fee to an organization promoting democracy in the region.

9   The USLBA seamlessly transitioned into the post-Gaddafi era after the colonel was overthrown in 2011. Its Web site deleted all references to him, and not long after his downfall, carried news about the arrival in the US for "urgent medical care" of two dozen wounded Libyan fighters. Never mind that they were wounded fighting the government of the association's former pal, Gaddafi.

6. The Lobbyists: Louisiana

1   They were outlawed earlier most everywhere else. Texas barred their use in 1969 and California in the mid-1960s.

2   Nor was Exxon's cause helped by Mark Krohn, the company's environmental consultant and witness, who was decimated by Stuart Smith, Grefer's attorney, on cross-examination. In addition to demonstrating that Krohn's company did a less-than-thorough job of examining Grefer's property in concluding that there was not much damage to it, Smith elicited from Krohn that his undergraduate degree in general science came from the University of the State of New York, an unaccredited institution where he took correspondence courses while in the navy; that he had dropped out of the New York State Maritime Academy because, he confessed, "I was spending too much time having too much fun," and that the certification he had won for having completed a course in the transportation of radioactive materials had